John Burks was formerly managing editor of *Rolling Stone* and is currently on the staff of the *San Francisco Examiner*. He is one of the most knowledgeable writers on popular music today.

Fred Ferretti is a member of the staff of the *New York Times*, joining the paper as a television critic-reporter in 1969 after working with the NBC News organization.

Len Fulton is a leading figure in the small press movement and has himself been a small press publisher for ten years *(Dustbooks)*. He currently serves as chairman of the Board of Directors of the Committee of Small Magazine Editors and Publishers.

John Gordon Burke is the associate editor of *American Libraries*, the official bulletin of the American Library Association.

PRINT, IMAGE AND SOUND

ESSAYS ON MEDIA

PRINT, IMAGE AND SOUND

ESSAYS ON MEDIA

John Gordon Burke, Editor

American Library Association
Chicago 1972

Library of Congress Cataloging in Publication Data
Main entry under title:

Print, image, and sound.

  Includes bibliographies.
  1. Mass media—Addresses, essays, lectures.
I. Burke, John Gordon, 1938–   ed. II. American
Library Association.
P87.P7   301.16′1′09046   70-39010
ISBN 0-8389-0122-0 (1972)

International Standard Book Number 0–8389–0122–0 (1972)

Library of Congress Catalog Card Number 70–39010

CONTENTS

INTRODUCTION
John Gordon Burke

PRINT, IMAGE AND SOUND is an attempt to bring both conceptual and bibliographical perspective to five areas of media in the 1960s. The social and political tumult of this period makes an analysis of this type difficult and perhaps valid only for a short time. If this is indeed true, then it is important for future historians to have this "perspective" on the 1960s, so that what seemed significant can be analyzed for the reasons which made it so. It is my belief, however, that this collection presents statements about film and popular music in the 1960s which will be valid for some time to come.

The media selected for analysis have been chosen from those necessary to consider—journalism, film, and popular music—and two potentially interesting areas, educational television and the little magazine. Other topics were considered for inclusion, but were decided against for a variety of reasons. And finally, poster art was excluded because it was related in a very basic way to popular music of the sixties. What remained are the five essays included here, representing both print and nonprint media.

In terms of our contributors, every effort was made to find a person intimately involved in the activities he was to write

1

about. To a certain extent, every collective "personal" effort fails, but I think given a proper understanding of the bibliography which accompanies each article, this anthology does bring into focus a number of important critical judgments. For example, James Ridgeway's statement, "The underground press opened up the press to ordinary people. That tendency won't be reversed," carries the weight of authority. And John Burks' opinion that popular music is historically rooted in both jazz and blues might at first seem untrue or at best a superficial point of view, but if you accept the fact that value judgments can be made about the music of the sixties, it carries an irrefutable logic.

The bibliographies are included to provide a framework through which the reader can locate for himself the conceptual dimensions of each essay's topic. They are selective and range in purpose from "illustrative of trends" to "comprehensive." Each bibliography is intended to be an integral part of the essay, and attempts to present information with which the reader can construct an analysis of the subject if he so chooses.

Special acknowledgment and appreciation are due several individuals in connection with this project. Marvin Kitman provided assistance with educational television and John Lux suggested a minimum of four titles for this anthology. Gerald Shields has also provided encouragement. These essays were commissioned and published under the auspices of the ALA Editorial Committee. They are reprinted in part from *American Libraries*.

THE NEW JOURNALISM

James Ridgeway

A new sort of journalism is taking shape in America. Most obviously it represents a reaction, even rebellion, to the established mass circulation press and to the culture and politics that press represents. But the papers and magazines which reflect this tendency are different from one another and they are apt to suddenly change or even disappear. Perhaps the best way to understand the new journalism is to look at some of the major influences.

Among the most important was the rise of *Ramparts* as a pioneering radical, counterculture mass circulation magazine. *Ramparts* was influential because of its style—hip San Francisco—and muckraking radical reports—Don Duncan's revelations of his life as a Green Beret in Vietnam, the CIA-NSA liaison, Diem's odd intrigues with Cardinal Spellman and the Vietnam lobby.

In the early 1960s *Ramparts* was a Catholic magazine with a circulation of four thousand. By 1968, when Warren Hinckle, a former publicity man, had done his best, the paper had a circulation of a quarter of a million and was tottering

James Ridgeway is an editor of *Ramparts* magazine.

3

towards bankruptcy with debts of more than one million dollars. In part, Hinckle made *Ramparts* by turning himself into a news item. During a domestic air strike, Hinckle was stranded in Chicago but had to get to New York. So he flew there via London. Taxis were too much trouble to hail, so Hinckle hired a chauffeur-driven limousine instead. He checked into the *Ramparts* suite at the Algonquin, then descended to do business from the bar. Outside in the lobby swooning groups of publishers, society ladies, and reporters would wait to be summoned to the table where Hinckle would describe the latest scoop in progress, such as getting the goods on LBJ, the Pope, NATO. On one hot tip *Ramparts'* editors seriously considered digging up a body buried in a Brooklyn grave in order to document a conspiracy theory. *Ramparts* seldom broke stories in the magazine, but more often announced the most prized exposés through advertisements in the *New York Times* or *Washington Post*. If the press of New York or Washington were otherwise occupied, the *Ramparts* public relations team would fly to Milwaukee or Cleveland, and give out the story there. *Ramparts* announced its CIA-NSA exposé in a *New York Times* ad. By the time the magazine itself appeared on the newsstand, its story seemed dull and dated when compared to the reams of material appearing in the newspapers. *Ramparts* also acted as tipster to reporters on major newspapers, offering them hot tid-bits in return for mentioning the magazine's name. In 1968, as the paper slid towards bankruptcy, Hinckle departed and launched *Scanlan's* monthly, which didn't catch fire in the same way *Ramparts* did and soon folded.

Ramparts had a great influence on other magazines and papers. It popularized muckraking and provided a model for the cloak and dagger "investigative reporting" teams established by newspapers after the CIA-NSA exposé. Dugald Sturmer, *Ramparts* art director, was employed by other magazines to improve their makeup. Jann Wenner, who launched the successful *Rolling Stone,* worked for *Ramparts* and possesses Hinckle's flair for advertising. *Ramparts* itself reorganized under the bankruptcy laws, and struggles along, a more stolid, serious publication.

Another magazine with a far more serious political influence than *Ramparts* is the *New Republic*. Under the editorship of Gilbert Harrison, the *New Republic* has built itself into a widely read political paper. It also exercises considerable political influence in Washington. In part, this is due to Harrison's own political interests which put him in close touch with liberal and moderate politicians. During the Democratic Administrations of Kennedy and Johnson, correspondents of the paper were well received in the offices of Administration leaders. Long before they were popularized in other papers, the *New Republic* wrote about and argued for auto and tire safety, and attacked environmental pollution. The *New Republic* first reported and analyzed the emergence of the New Left, and provided the early, systematic criticisms and reports on the Vietnam war. The paper is widely read by political leaders in Washington, but also finds its way down into the layers of the government bureaucracy. In some respects the *New Republic* has shed its liberal intellectual aura and is now the political paper of the "New Class, those professionals and technocrats who backed McCarthy or Kennedy, and who in 1970, found themselves turning populist with Ralph Nader."

Surely the most important influence in journalism has been the rise of the *Wall Street Journal* to the position of a commanding national paper with a reputation very much like *LeMonde* or the *Times* of London. The *Journal,* with its conservative origins, is an economic success because of shrewd foresight in taking advantage of electronic publishing and because it offers most parts of the country fast news of the stock markets. But the paper's reputation is based on the news coverage, which attempts to explain economic and cultural events briefly and clearly. Unlike so many other papers and magazines, the *Journal* reporters explain events to nonspecialist readers. Readers of the *Journal* take the paper seriously because, whatever their politics, they trust its judgment.

The most spectacular occurrence in recent journalism was the overnight emergence of the underground press. There are about two hundred underground papers with an estimated

5

circulation of six million or more. The background of the business is the Liberation News Service (LNS), headquartered in New York City. LNS was begun in 1967 by Marshall Bloom and Ray Mungo, graduates of Amherst and Boston University respectively. Both had been editors of student newspapers, and Bloom was meant to head up the United States Student Press Association, but he was deemed to be too radical and never got the job. In its early days LNS was more hip than political, and in 1968 after the service moved to New York from Washington, a bitter battle broke out among the staff over the proper political course for the service. In the end, one faction led by Mungo and Bloom made off to a Massachusetts farm with the money and equipment. The other group stayed in New York, formed a collective, and began to publish a news service. For a time there were two LNS. But soon Bloom and Mungo gave up. (Mungo now farms and writes books. Bloom committed suicide in November 1969.)

LNS offers a radical critique of American institutions. The service now mails two packets of news a week to eight hundred subscribers. Underground papers pay twenty dollars a month, overground papers and institutions more. An LNS packet, usually containing twenty pages or so, includes reports, political analysis, comics, cartoons, photographs, recipes. The October 8, 1970 packet, for instance, contains the second part of a long interview with Leila Khaled, in which she describes her decision to become a guerrilla. There are several reports on the various Panther trials under way. There is an unusual report released by the Tupamaros of an interview between their members and Dan Mitrione, the U.S. police expert working in Uruguay. (After the interview was made, the Tupamaros killed Mitrione.) A note from Timothy Leary announces his escape from prison and warmly endorses the Weathermen. The packet includes an account of Jimi Hendrix's death and a report on the Young Lords with special reference to their attitude towards women. This packet would have reached most underground editors before the established press published the news, and indeed, the big papers probably picked up the Leary note from LNS.

The LNS reports from abroad are often interesting and useful. The correspondents tend to cull the best from the foreign press, then add their own first-hand accounts. In some instances established foreign correspondents write directly for the service. LNS concentrates on the different revolutionary fronts and has run stories from correspondents behind guerrilla lines in Jordan. Just as Nixon was moving into Cambodia, LNS was distributing an excellent report on the Indochina war by Jacques DeCornoy, the *LeMonde* correspondent who had recently returned from the Far East. The LNS piece was an excerpt from a radio interview its correspondents had made with DeCornoy, and provided the sort of historical and political background on the war which was not available in U.S. papers at the time. LNS covers the underground at home with a continuing stream of reports and analysis. It provided extensive coverage of the university revolts. However, the service is spotty on economic news and relies on radical rhetoric instead.

LNS views the news as propaganda. Just as *Time* for so long never ran articles critical of the Vietnam policies, LNS probably would not run articles suggesting the "revolution" is disintegrating. But taking its political line into account, an inevitability with any paper or magazine, LNS provides a useful source of information on opposition and revolutionary politics.

The Underground Press Syndicate (UPS) was formed in 1966 in Phoenix and it serves as a sort of underground publishers conglomerate. Tom Forcade, the energetic leader, describes UPS as an "appliance. It does not attempt to speak for any underground paper's political or cultural views or act as their conscience. UPS is part of the plumbing which does things which somebody has to do, but nobody wants to. We are an administrative group, a research organization, a watchdog agency, and an information bureau. We are not the national headquarters of a political party, nor are the papers chapters." Membership in UPS costs a one-time twenty-five dollars. The association helps members by microfilming their back issues and selling an underground press library to libraries. It then pays the different papers their share of the

7

microfilming take. UPS created and runs an advertising service which provides a substantial amount of income to many underground papers. Intertribal News Service (FRINS), a biweekly news packet, is published by the Free Ranger Tribe, which consists of some UPS members. FRINS goes out to underground papers but also is sent to radio stations in the hope of developing an underground consciousness among them. Members of UPS promise not to copyright articles. Copyright is a form of property and UPS members are opposed to it.

It is difficult to keep track of the different underground papers because they come and go so fast. But over the past few years certain papers stand out. They include the *Old Mole,* Cambridge; *Great Speckled Bird,* Atlanta; *RAT,* New York; and *San Francisco Express Times.* Others in the same vein are *Kaleidoscope,* Milwaukee; *Seed,* Chicago; *NOLA Express,* New Orleans; and *Space City,* Houston. These papers have been successful at reflecting the interests of their communities, which means they have brought together the freak, anarchist, and political revolutionary constituencies within the counter culture. Many of the most interesting and most enduring papers are southern: *The Bird, Space City, NOLA Express, Dallas Notes, Rag.* (The original *RAT* was begun by Jeff Shero, a Texan.) They have an easy, native populist-radical quality which other papers strive to imitate but somehow fail to achieve. Writers for these papers are deft at parody, and the papers are wildly funny. They include a bit of muckraking, and infrequently discuss the power structure in imitation of C. Wright Mills.

People argue about the antecedents of the underground papers. The *Village Voice* is the oldest of the papers. John Wilcock, who wrote a column for the *Voice* on the avant-garde, helped the underground papers develop. He quit the *Voice* to launch the *East Village Other,* and then went on to begin *Other Scenes.* The *Berkeley Barb* was widely imitated during the 1960s and greatly admired for the Dr. Hippocrates column. The *Los Angeles Free Press* proved one could make a lot of money in the underground business. But the most important single influence on the underground press was provided by Paul Krassner and his paper, the *Realist*. Influenced by his friend, Lenny Bruce, Krassner really first pulled together the freak-anarchist tendencies.

While it is usual to separate "cultural" from "political" papers this is a dubious distinction, since all publications tend to reflect in one way or another radical or revolutionary politics. Thus, in the summer of 1969, the papers were given over to the split-up in SDS, then to the development of Weatherman, and to repression of the Panthers and other radicals. By the spring of 1970, the underground press was consumed with the Women's Liberation matter. Some papers, such as *RAT*, were taken over by women; others such as the *Old Mole* went through painful reexaminations and emerged promising to struggle against male chauvanism. ("The *Old Mole* announces that it will no longer accept manuscripts or letters that use language such as emasculation, castration, balls to mean courage, letters addressed 'Dear Sir' or 'Gentlemen' or other examples of male supremacist language.")

Women's papers have sprung up all around the country—there are at least twenty-five of them now publishing—and they are the center of attention in the underground press. These papers generally have a distinctly puritanical cast and in one way or another argue for developing a separatist movement. In doing so they reflect the politics of the radical lesbians, who are the most energetic and interesting group within the movement at this writing. The papers are often much the same in content; they include reports or short stories describing some grizzly sex act the author has been made to endure by a male chauvanist pig. *It Ain't Me Babe,* the Berkeley paper, told how an exotic dancer had come to the Women's Liberation and told how she had been made to perform unnatural and degrading sex acts with men at a bachelor's party held in honor of a groom before his wedding. The women decided to expose this sort of thing, and wrote up broadsides describing the "rape" and handed them out to the members of the wedding party.

The letters are a bit less propagandistic: the *RAT* carried a long letter from a woman who said her new lesbian lover was just as manipulative and devious as her former boy friend. She had tossed him out for the sake of the movement, but for what good.

Women, a quarterly magazine published in Baltimore, is one of the most widely regarded liberation publications. The contents of the Fall 1970 issue tend to reflect a good deal of the thinking of the women's press. That issue contains a literary analysis of Dickens, Joyce, Hemingway, Faulkner, and Shakespeare which concludes they all in one way or another took an uninformed, male chauvanistic view of women. Virginia Woolf is viewed as a humanist, although the author says Woolf was obviously intelligent. Louisa May Alcott is warmly praised. Her heroines often did not marry. According to the author, this may have been because Alcott was influenced by her home life. There her father kept her mother in a state of abject captivity. *Women* goes on to attack capitalist fairy tales as thinly disguised male supremacist propaganda. (Snow White cleaned house for not one but *seven* dwarfs.) In an editorial *Women* says art is for the rich and has no meaning for the masses. Thus, art should be redefined and given new political direction as part of a collective enterprise.

Most of the women's papers follow the approach of *Women,* offering bits and pieces of politics and history, looked at from the feminist perspective, and arguing for a collective movement. The papers generally reflect the interests of what appear to be upper-class, white intellectuals.

Among the most interesting work to come out of the underground press are the research reports. These emanate from various groups or collectives and generally aim to provide a more detailed understanding of American institutions from a radical point of view. Oftentimes the research is carried out as part of an attempt to organize political actions.

The North American Congress on Latin America (NACLA) is the most formidable of these groups. NACLA was formed after the Dominican invasion by a handful of young people in an effort to develop some sort of coherent analysis of U.S. foreign policy in Latin America. The organization has offices in New York and Berkeley and publishes a newsletter as well as a periodic press packet for the underground papers. The *NACLA Newsletter,* published ten times a year with fifteen hundred subscribers in the United States, Latin American, and Europe, carries useful and not otherwise available reports about U.S. operations in Latin America. In past issues *NACLA Newsletter* ran thorough accounts of the way in which the Catholic church operates in Latin America and the Hanna industrial empire's control over mines in Brazil as well as its power over the finances of the Republican party. NACLA has published details of the Bank of America's agribusiness involvement in Latin America and described how the big U.S. communications companies tied up communications in Latin countries. NACLA also provides special reports on university ties with the Pentagon. More recently it publicized the relationships between police departments and universities in the United States.

Recently NACLA began publishing a packet of news about Latin America for the underground papers. This sort of service, offered free to papers which can't afford to pay, is unique. Most daily papers and newsmagazines in the United States have, at best, spotty coverage of Latin America. NACLA's service is comprehensive, and it is one of the reasons the group's work is so highly respected within the CIA.

NACLA staff members will consult with local groups on request, and NACLA helped establish Africa Research Group in Cambridge. Like NACLA, Africa Research Group makes available periodic reports and studies on U.S. and European influences in Africa.

The *HEALTH/PAC Bulletin,* published monthly by the Health Policy Advisory Center, New York City, offers the same sort of thorough research on the medical profession, with special concentration on developing radical empires—complexes of hospitals, doctors, and corporations within the city of New York. *HEALTH/PAC* is at the center of a movement which aims to turn over governance of the health industry—clinics, hospitals, delivery systems—to the communities most directly affected.

Another research group producing interesting material is the Council on Economic Priorities. With offices in Washington and New York City, the council produces books and short studies of various industries. These include an examination of firms which sell antipersonnel weapons and a recent investigation of pollution problems in the paper industry. The reports are factual and contain financial data which must be interpreted.

Finally, there is the series of studies on government and industry made by Nader's Raiders, the young attorneys who work under Ralph Nader's general supervision. The best of these are published as books. Two which come immediately to mind are the *Chemical Feast* by James Turner and *Our Vanishing Air* by John Esposito. One is a study of chemicals in food, the other an angry indictment of the nation's air pollution programs.

Underground papers are cheap to produce, which is one of the main reasons there are so many of them. Any typewriter equipped with a carbon ribbon can be used to set type. Despite the alleged right-wing politics of printers' unions, the papers are printed cheaply and quickly. And papers with intricate drawings of bombs, replete with dirty stories and pictures of people engaged in various sex acts, are printed all the time.

Robert Glessing, author of *The Underground Press in America,* a recent and excellent study of the underground press, describes the printing cost of an average paper in some detail:

> Most underground papers operate on a total budget of five hundred to one thousand dollars per issue. The expenditures of the San Francisco *Good Times* with a press run of twelve thousand copies is closer to the average underground newspaper—$20 per thousand, sixteen-page papers plus $6.50 per page for negatives and plates. There is no make-ready charge for runs of over five thousand, and a $35 base fee is charged for color plus $2.50 per thousand. Most publishers in this study charge $50 base fee for color plus the $2.50 per thousand. Thus the average printing bill for publishers of *Good Times* is $350 to $400 "up front" per issue unless they run color. "Up front" is a term used by printers of underground

papers indicating they must be paid in advance of publication.

If a paper wants to look really professional, it may rent
an IBM composer for about $150 a month. This machine is
in effect an electric typewriter with a coding device which
enables the operator to set justified lines (that is, even lines
of type) in a variety of different type fonts. This machinery
is made by several companies, but the IBM system generally
works very well indeed, and unlike other firms, IBM provides
free and fast service when there is a breakdown. The composer provides an underground paper with all the capabilities
of a linotype machine for a fraction of the cost.

The key to success of underground papers lies in their distribution system. In most large cities and towns distribution
of papers and magazines—even books—is controlled by one
or two major companies. These operators are not usually
willing to endanger their monopoly by selling papers which
may be attacked by the police as pornographic, thereby en-
dangering their business. As a practical matter, whatever
the politics involved, it is a terrible problem getting distribu-
tors to handle underground papers. Sometimes they want
money in advance; they always are inefficient, late in pay-
ment. The underground press gets around this by having
established an alternative street sales force. It depends on the
street culture for youngsters who come into the paper's office,
buy one hundred copies for half the price, and then hawk
them on the corner for the full cover price. In some cities
underground papers have such widespread distribution operations that there are wholesalers who get a few cents per
issue for hauling bundles to far-away spots where youngsters
pick them up for street sales. Thus, every successful underground paper is sold with a distribution mechanism fully
equal to that of the biggest daily. The papers appeal to the
counterculture community, but they also are widely sold to
straight people because they generally include personal sex
ads, a smattering of pornography, and, in recent months,
exciting adventure stories about dashing Weatherman gueril-
las. They also have good comics. Without the sharply reduced printing costs and development of a street sales force,

it is doubtful that underground papers could have become so widespread.

Alternative mechanisms for distributing papers seem pretty grim as our experience with *Hard Times* tends to suggest. When we were still editors at the *New Republic* in 1967, Andrew Kopkind and I joined with other journalists in attempting to lay out plans for a national newsmagazine with radical politics. Attempts to raise money for such a project were futile. (At the time wealthy liberals were splitting away from radicals because of the Israeli War and beginnings of black separatist politics.) Instead we joined Robert Sherrill in launching a four-page weekly paper—really a newsletter—called *Mayday*. Sherrill subsequently left this paper, and its name was changed to *Hard Times* because of a trademark dispute. *Hard Times* attempted to carry muckraking on power politics as well as coverage of the revolutionary-freak scene as it unfolded here and abroad. Initially the paper was warmly backed by Richard Grossman and Michael Loeb of Grossman Publishers. They invested some money themselves and persuaded others to join in. Without their help we probably would never have been able to start *Hard Times*. (Incidentally, while we talked of doing books with them, the only book published was with World, not Grossman.)

Hard Times was designed by Sam Antupit to look like a newspaper. Production costs ran to about five hundred dollars per issue, including three hundred dollars for printing and mailing. Our printing costs were higher than they might have been because we used a good grade of paper, and also because *Hard Times* was sent out second-class mail. While second class is the least expensive method of mailing, and intended to help subsidize small publications such as ours, it necessitates special sorting and bundling, which with a small list runs up costs. Our circulation eventually reached between five and six thousand subscribers, and almost all of them were solicited by direct-mail promotion. Originally we had wanted to stay clear of direct mail because of the pitch. But it was unavoidable. The paper—with no pictures or comics, no sex ads, only four pages, directed at a national not local audience—never sold much on newsstands. Magazine advertising brought in a few subscribers, but not enough to build a subscription list. Our paper probably never would have been especially popular: It wasn't acid-rock, or street-fighting radical, or liberal intelligentsia. We tried to deal with these different tendencies and, in the process, to develop a sort of coherent radical analysis of the society. The point is, the paper never appealed to a clearly defined set of people. We fell into direct mail and that process very largely ruined the paper.

It costs between $75 and $90 per 1,000 to mail out a direct-mail promotion. The usual commercial return on such a mailing is 1 percent. (The direct-mail people will tell you the return can be much higher, but in my experience, these claims are not to be taken with any seriousness.) With a 1 percent return it's necessary to send out letters to 100,000 people to get 1,000 subscribers. At the very least this will cost about $7,000. The return, if you're lucky, will just cover the costs. The paper then must foot the bill in servicing the subscriber for a year. We found at one point that it cost us $7.50 for every subscriber we were getting through direct mail. In effect, the paper pays the direct-mail promoter a fee, about $7,000, for 1,000 subscribers. The second year around, things get a little better, and perhaps 50 percent of those who subscribed the first year will resubscribe. Thus, to hold level with 5,000 subscribers, it is necessary to promote to 250,000 people every year. After awhile the paper may catch on and slowly build up of its own accord, but this takes time. You probably have to count on holding for at least 5 years before that process takes hold.

For awhile the direct-mail business produces some results. If he is shrewd, the promotion man will put you on to lists of magazines with similar orientation, in our case left-liberal. But after a year, these names are worn out, and it's necessary to revert to gimmicks, such as the famous-person letter, a whining plea by some famous person, sent along to susceptible population groups, executives making over $20,000 living in the Upper East Side of Manhattan, for example. We began sending out famous-person letters during the spring of 1970. In fact, we sent out several different famous-person letters, all signed by Dustin Hoffman—who all too kindly allowed us to use his name—to different hot lists, and waited for the money to pour in. It didn't. I even sent out a letter to librarians. It was written by the direct-mail man, who claimed he had a long experience in the game and had been successful at putting to gether just the right sort of pitch: honest, sincere, titillating, blah, blah. I thought it sounded pretty silly, but he insisted, and the letter was dispatched to 10,000 libraries. We waited breathlessly for the response. There were about 10 replies in all.

From time to time we sought to enlarge our audience by combining with another paper, actually merging with publications or making some sort of joint mailing arrangement—for example, tying together two biweekly publications so that a subscriber would get two different papers for the price of one. *Ramparts* was interested, and we ended up creating a section called *Hard Times* in it. They agreed to service our subscribers, and we became editors of that magazine.

While the Liberation News Service reports are a great help to editors of underground papers, they also have an unfortunate effect. The papers which rely on LNS imitate one another much as the big daily papers repeat themselves in relying on the wire services. There is little local reporting, one of the major reasons for beginning underground papers. Some of the underground papers do reflect the interests of freak or radical communities, but many of them don't do that either and are merely local mouth organs for revolutionary solidarity as laid down by LNS. When the LNS is badly wrong as it was in exaggerating the influence of first the "Movement" and then the "Revolution," the papers which rely on it look foolish.

Only on rare occasions do underground papers perform the sort of reporting and analytic functions as did *I. F. Stone's Weekly*. This sort of reporting which generates a coherent political analysis is rarely found, and then most often in small, local weekly papers of what radicals would despairingly refer to as "liberal" or populist persuasion. Unhappily, the great interest in the alternate press hasn't helped these papers much at all. Some of them are very good indeed and badly need assistance. One is the *Mountain Eagle*, the Whitesburg, Kentucky, weekly. With Tom Gish as editor, the *Eagle* has tirelessly crusaded in behalf of the people of Appalachia, and especially those in eastern Kentucky. Gish fought strip mining, argued for safety in deep coal mines, and for the past ten years has acted as a one-man public relations agent to persuade reporters from national papers to come down and write about the hell of Appalachia. Gish and his wife Pat put the *Eagle* out by themselves, and recently Tom Bethell gave them a hand with hard-nosed reporting on the coal industry. Bethell now has begun a biweekly on the coal industry called *Coal Patrol*, and it is an excellent source of information on the machinations of the business in Appalachia. In San Francisco the *Bay Guardian* comes out once every six weeks, and it is full of muckraking on ecology, the electric light monopoly, and other West Coast industries. Ronnie Dugger publishes his investigations in the *Texas Observer*, which has a national reputation for its liberal-minded reporting on the South. In Boise, Idaho, the *Intermountain Observer* is a fine, local weekly crammed with first-hand reports on politics and odd customs of the mountains. The *New Mexico Review*, published in Santa Fe, offers good first-hand reports on land exploitation in the Southwest. Judged by any usual political measure, these papers in their reports and analyses are far more radical than most underground papers.

Then there are other recent journalistic departures which can't be lumped into any particular category. The brief emergence of Dispatch News Service represented one nearly successful effort to break the hold of UPI and AP on established newspapers, and in the process provide some fresh, interesting work. That occurred when David Opst, manager of Dispatch, published Seymour Hersh's exposé of the My Lai massacre. At this writing, Dispatch was sending out stories to seventy major newspapers and mailing a weekly packet to colleges as well. Opst also packages books and acts as writers' agent. He arranged to distribute stories from Pacific News Service, a Berkeley outfit which gathers news in the Far East, especially from within Communist-held portions of Indochina. Even with all this activity, Opst is hard pressed to make ends meet.

17

Newspapers pay between $35 and $75 for a 750-word story, and that must be split fifty-fifty with the writer. In 1970, Opst sought outside financing, and he hopes book packaging schemes will help keep things going.

Since ecology became a big issue, a string of hysteria papers has appeared. Most attempt to exploit the issue and are pretty trivial. The best of the lot is *Environment*, formerly called *Scientist and Citizen*. The articles are well done, informative, and generally appear well in advance of reports on the same subject in other papers. Reading *Environment* is a good way for an ordinary person, with no special training in these matters, to keep abreast of and understand the complexities of ecological problems.

Over the next ten years there is likely to be more of an effort towards building up local papers, whether they be small town, college, or underground. If anything, this tendency will be reinforced because of the spreading interest in environmental issues and because of an enthusiasm for populist-style politics.

Economic forces in publishing provide compelling reasons for not creating more big slick magazines. The costs of publishing and distributing these monsters are already enormous. There is little room for maneuvering in cutting costs: Printing plants are unionized, and the unions are locked in a struggle to preserve the business as they know it. The national distribution mechanisms are virtual monopolies, accessible only to those with money and conforming ideas. More important, advertisers are at least temporarily shifting away from mass circulation papers and magazines (note the decline in ad revenue by *Life*) and experimenting with smaller magazines and papers which are directed to special groups in the population. Now that the post office threatens to abandon subsidy to publishers in the form of reduced postage rates, publishers are turning to private carriers, and, in all likelihood, future entrance into publishing will require even more capital than it already does.

Underground papers are momentarily in decline, influenced both by the break-up of the Movement and by the recession which has sharply reduced advertising revenue from record companies. If the Vietnam war ends, these papers may disappear at an even faster rate. There may be a reversion to newsletters, such as Stone's, but as indicated above, this is a fairly expensive business, and with postal subsidies disappearing the future does not look bright. Dispatch, NACLA, and LNS suggest the possibilities of covering a mass market of local papers with national reporting.

It is always possible that the new journalism will turn away from print media altogether and go into some electronic form —radio, TV, cable television. But this is fairly costly, especially so if the stations seek to do their own programming. Any move in this direction would depend on some sort of wide-scale government financing, and that does not appear imminent.

Most important, the underground press opened up the press to ordinary people. That tendency won't be reversed. Journalism, the very best journalism, is not a business for professional technicians, but ought rather to be the natural evocation of every citizen in a democracy. And in that sense the underground radicals have created the basis for real revolutionary change.

Bibliography

The following is a listing of news services, reports, papers, and topical publications of more than routine interest:

NEWS SERVICES

Liberation News Service, 160 Claremont Ave., New York, NY; twice a week, $240 a month for underground papers. The backbone of the underground press and an invaluable service.

Free Ranger Intertribal News Service, Box 26, Village Station, New York, NY 10014. Produced periodically in cooperation with the Underground Press Syndicate at the same address. Reprints features of interest from the underground press.

REPORTS

NACLA Newsletter, P.O. Box 57, Cathedral Park Station, New York, NY 10025; $5, 10 times a year. Interesting reports, analysis of U.S. involvement in Latin America. Also special reports, including a look at university ties with the Pentagon, and developing relations between universities and police departments. Also a student's handbook laying out, step by step, how to research his university and its relations with various other institutions.

Health/PAC Bulletin, published by the Health Policy Advisory Center, Inc., 17 Murray Street, New York, NY 10007; $7, monthly. Reports on the health industry, with special reference to New York City.

Africa Research Group, Box 213, Cambridge, MA 02138. Periodic reports on imperialism in Africa.

PAPERS

NOLA Express, Box 2342, New Orleans, LA 70116; $3, biweekly. New Orleans community underground, all-around opposition newspaper.

Space City, 1217 Wichita, Houston, TX 77004; $5, biweekly. Underground opposition in Houston.

Great Speckled Bird, 253 North Ave. N.E., Atlanta, GA ·30308; $6, weekly. Widely imitated; one of the best underground community papers.

Rising Up Angry, Box 3746, Merchandise Mart, Chicago, IL 60654; $5, monthly. An attempt at a revolutionary paper.

Liberated Guardian, 14 Cooper Square, New York, NY 10003; $10, weekly. Revolutionary.

El Grito del Norte, Box 466, Fairview St., Espanola, NM 87532; $4, biweekly. Articles in both English and Spanish. Chicano resistance.

WIN, 339 Lafayette St., New York, NY 10012; $5, bimonthly. Published by the War Resisters League. "Peace and Freedom through nonviolent action."

The Black Panther, Ministry of Information, Box 2967, Custom House, San Francisco, CA 94126; $7.50, weekly. Party paper.

Seed, 2551 N. Halsted, Chicago, IL 60614; $6, biweekly. Underground, hip-radical.

Iconoclast, P.O. Box 7013, Dallas, TX 75209; $10, weekly. Radical/freak. Succeeds *Dallas Notes*.

New Mexico Review and Legislative Journal, P.O. Box 2328, Santa Fe, NM 87501; $5, monthly. Muckraking reports on Southwest land development.

Texas Observer, 504 W. 24th St., Austin, TX 78705; $7, biweekly. Texas politics from a liberal point of view.

San Francisco Bay Guardian, 1070 Bryant St., San Francisco, CA 94103; $5, every six weeks or so. Muckraking, liberal politics.

Maine Times, 13 Main St., Topsham, ME 04086; $7, weekly. Excellent environmental reporting.

Point of View, 2150 Rexwood, Cleveland, OH 44118; $5, biweekly. Radical reporting on Cleveland and industrial Midwest.

ENVIRONMENT

Environment, P.O. Box 755, Bridgeton, MO 63044; $8.50, monthly. An original reporting on evironmental problems. A splendid magazine.

Mother Earth News, 1899 Hubbard Road, North Madison, OH 44057; $5, bimonthly. "Heavy emphasis is placed on alternative life styles . . . working with nature and doing more with less."

WOMEN

Women, 3028 Greenmount Ave., Baltimore, MD 21218; $4, quarterly. Political analysis and literary criticism.

It Ain't Me Babe, 1126 Addison, Berkeley, CA 94701; $6, every three weeks. Reports from the West Coast women's movement.

Off Our Backs, P.O. Box 4859, Cleveland Park Station, Washington, DC 20008; $6, biweekly. Down-to-earth reporting.

EDUCATIONAL TELEVISION

Fred Ferretti

Educational television in the 1950s tried to be faithful to its name, atempting with conscious effort to be an educational medium; culturally oriented, proper, uplifting, tending to bring the concepts of the lecture hall into the living room. Only recently has the medium learned that it cannot teach that way, that learning from television is not deliberate and conscious, but a gradual process of assimilation of information and attitudes.

In the 1960s educational television began breaking out of its narrow didactic cocoon. Marshall McLuhan, the electronic philosopher, said it first—the medium itself is the message— and television discovered that he was right. It tried to entertain as it taught, to amuse with its message. In 1967, Congress passed the Public Broadcasting Act and changed educational TV to "public" television, legislating to it a broader scope, encouraging public television and radio stations to think of themselves not as isolated and insulated local broadcasters, but as parts of a fledgling network. And on at least one public

Fred Ferretti joined the staff of the *New York Times* in 1969 as television critic-reporter and currently serves on the general staff.

television program, "Sesame Street," the wedding of learning and TV was consummated with wit, style, and expertise.

In the 1970s public television will have to learn to be dynamic and adaptive, a real alternative to commercial broadcasting, by always keeping an eye on its "public" responsibility. William H. Siemering, general manager of WBFO, on the Buffalo campus of the State University of New York, has outlined public broadcasting's mission as well as anyone: "We must be academically respectable to receive institutional support but broadly based to receive public acceptance; we must have professional production to be competitive with the neighboring stations but retain enough solid content to be socially relevant. We must use the medium imaginatively but with one-tenth of the resources of commercial stations."

With the creation last year of the Public Broadcast Service, small stations have found themselves part of a nationwide network and have needed only a videotape receiver to accumulate libraries of slickly produced, network-quality programs. This development will certainly change the face of public broadcasting and make it difficult for small stations to keep their preeminent mission in front of them—service to their local communities, the communities which they were licensed to serve. With the network will come changes in public television's alignments. In the 1960s there was really but one program source for the nation's public TV stations—National Educational Television in New York; in the 1970s there will be numerous sources of network programming, a recommendation made by the Carnegie Commission on Public Television in 1966.

These other network production centers have already begun to operate. In addition to WNET in New York, there now exist KQED in San Francisco; KCET in Los Angeles; WETA in Washington, D.C.; WTTW in Chicago; WGBH in Boston; WQED in Pittsburgh; and the Children's Television Workshop in New York.

These stations and other centers around the country were responsible for such programs as "Sesame Street," "Hollywood Television Theatre," "Black Frontier," "Realities," "NET Playhouse," "Soul!," "Kukla, Fran and Ollie," "Mister Rogers'

23

Neighborhood," "Flick Out," "Fanfare," "San Francisco Mix," "The Great American Dream Machine," "Homewood," "Black Journal," "Book Beat," "The Advocates," "The French Chef," and "Vanishing Wilderness."

Many of these programs were made possible only because of the increased support that Congress has given to public broadcasting through annual appropriations. This year $30 million was allocated to public broadcasting, to be distributed through the Corporation for Public Broadcasting (CPB), as well as $5 million more in matching funds. In addition, the Ford Foundation has continued to support heavily specific public television programs and projects, including "Newsrooms" in several cities and the creation of a local-network production center in New York City, the Educational Broadcasting Corporation, which now incorporates NET and the educational TV channel there, Channel 13, whose call letters were changed to WNET.

It is this continued enlargement of public television's political and program base that is causing concern in some sectors of the medium. Critics of the network formation claim that continual congressional funding on an annual basis will rob public television of its autonomy and independence. One such critic is Fred W. Friendly, former president of news for the Columbia Broadcasting System and now television consultant to the Ford Foundation.

Mr. Friendly, testifying before the Senate subcommittee on communications four years ago, on behalf of permanent funding of public TV, said, "I am not so hungry for [federal funds] that I am willing to say 'I don't care where the money comes from, or how, as long as we get it.' " He went on to say that he believed federal funds—either appropriations or trust funds were appropriate for public television facilities, "But I am sure that we must avoid at all costs any situation in which budgets for news and public affairs programming would be appropriated or even approved by any branch of the Federal Government. Even the most distinguished and courageous Board of Trustees could not insulate such programs from the budget and appropriation process."

Mr. Friendly's concerns are shared by many news and public affairs producers, who see with an increase in federal monies a decrease in their independence and editorial responsibility. This contention is denied, however, by the two men who preside over the two dominant public television organizations—John W. Macy, Jr., president of the Corporation for Public Broadcasting, and Hartford N. Gunn, Jr., president of the Public Broadcasting Service (PBS).

These men point to the increased production, both locally and nationally, of news-oriented programming and the increased support being lent to the stations with CPB funds. As examples Mr. Macy points to the $2.1 million given to NET to support "Black Journal," "NET Journal," and "NET Playhouse"; to the $1 million given to WGBH–Boston and KCET–Los Angeles for production of "The Advocates"; to WTTW–Chicago for "Book Beat," "Just Jazz," and "Kukla, Fran and Ollie"; and to the financial support given "World Press" at San Francisco's KQED and "Washington Week in Review" at WETA–Washington.

In addition, CPB cites presentation of the first complete criminal trial to be televised, "The City and County of Denver vs. Lauren R. Watson," as well as its coverage of "Honor America Day" and "Earth Day" and its participation in a four-network "Conversation with President Nixon" and in the President's State of Union message.

The debate over whether recurrent annual government funding of public broadcasting automatically carries with it governmental intervention in the internal affairs of public broadcasters can be expected to continue throughout the 70s. But as the programs which have emerged thus far in the current decade reflect, the wishes of most of the local stations are being carried out.

In November of 1969, on the threshold of a new decade, the country's Educational Television Stations, a division of the National Association of Educational Broadcasters, held a conference on programming goals. ETS board secretary Lloyd Kaiser and ETS executive director Chalmers Marquis introduced the conference with a joint statement:

Public TV is what happens to people because programs are put on the screen. Unless public broadcasting makes a significant difference in the lives of viewers, it simply will not, and should not, survive. To what purposes do we connect stations, foster production capabilities, seek out programs? . . . At the ETS Conference of April 1968, station managers shared ideas for programs in specific response to minority group problems. Since then, public television stations have presented thousands of hours of new programs for and by minority groups, and we have new evidence of their effectiveness.

Station managers stressed the need for more local responsibility and control of programming at the April, 1969, ETS Program Conference. Managers particularly emphasized the need for more local news analysis. There have been many efforts in this direction since then . . . . At the October, 1969, NET meeting, managers heard CPB President John Macy cite national needs in the fields of nutrition and health, population control, law enforcement, and the special problems of children.

The two ETS officers cited other conferences at which public broadcasting priorities had been discussed: "These are the comments and actions until now. What are our public TV priorities for the future? America's PTV stations clearly have a responsibility in helping to shape and satisfy their community's priorities. We believe we can assist one another in weighing these priorities—and determining how we can help meet them with public television's resources. It is to these public TV goals that this Conference is dedicated."

The results of the conference were highly significant, and the decisions made in Washington that November will be reflected in the public broadcasting programming of the 1970s.

Given as the most important program priority for the medium was covering local public issues—presenting local candidates for public office, covering elections "using local resources, local tie-ins, event-oriented programs, involvement programs, local crises." The conference finding was that in all discussions of the coverage of local issues "the vital thread of increasing local citizen participation" ran, as did the necessity for public broadcasting to provide "citizens with the political sophistication necessary to act responsibly in that process."

Citizen participation in broadcasting—and the participation takes many forms—burgeoned in the late 1960s. It will be a hallmark of the public broadcasting medium in this decade. The conference saw this participation on several levels: in the issues to be discussed—drugs, pollution, Vietnam, tax reform, race problems, Indian affairs, transportation, the elderly, law and the police, and housing; in the amount of news to be presented; in the explanations of existing government services; and in the techniques used to ensure this participation—documentaries, studio feedback sessions, live debates, coverage of city councils, state legislatures, school boards, and community events.

Omitted was one aspect of this participation which will be most important in the future: the involvement of the community in the decision-making processes of the broadcasters and the stations, a virtual advise and consent process. Community boards with advisory or policy-making authority in the fields of education, health, community planning, housing, and poverty programs have been created in cities around the country. And in several cities, most notably Jackson, Mississippi, and Atlanta, Georgia, community residents act as monitors and advisers to television and radio stations. Only recently have community boards been able to achieve changes in public policy and to alter decision making. This aspect of citizen participation will become most important in the near future of public broadcasting.

Of the specific subjects discussed by the conference, the environment rated highest in interest and concern. The member stations agreed that they had to help create "a national passion" for reclamation of the American environment, which they called "a critical survival problem." Of equal interest was the question of overpopulation.

The conferees agreed that an increase in the quantity and quality of children's programs was third in the list of priorities. It is in this area that public broadcasting has had its greatest effect, not only with the onset of "Sesame Street" but also earlier with such fare as "Mister Rogers' Neighborhood" and "Hodgepodge Lodge." But it was "Sesame Street" with its imaginative graphics, its amusing use of repetition and of Madison Avenue commercial techniques, its rapid pace, its use of commercial TV argot, and its happy propensity for not talking down to children, which won all the prizes and gathered the imitators. In commercial television there is not an executive in children's programming who is not borrowing "Sesame Street" tidbits for forthcoming programs. The Children's Television Workshop is currently at work on a new series aimed at increasing reading skills for youngsters already in school ("Sesame Street" is aimed at preschoolers) and has discussed other learning-oriented programs. CTW's continuing problem, as it is for the whole range of public broadcasting projects, is continued financing, although the Workshop has an easier time of it than other production centers because of its wide acceptance and favorable critical reception.

Programming for youth, aged 12 to 25, followed as the ETS conference's next priority. This was a particularly encouraging note, not because the conference came up with concrete programming ideas—which it did not—but because it at least addressed itself to the issue, which has been and continues to be a thorny one for all broadcasters, public or commercial. It is a fact ascertained by sociologists who have studied TV watching—who watches and why—that adolescents and young adults do not watch more TV than adults, but they watch different things.

They watch comedy of all kinds, but fewer news and documentary programs than do adults. They do *not* watch in significant numbers programs designed specifically for them, such as dance-party programs. A recent Center for Urban Education study found that adolescents think that television gives illustrations of life which they considered relevant to themselves; that they use TV as an antidepressant; and that they are excited by the medium to a greater degree than adults. Some of those in the study, about one-third, said that they found television helpful with their school work and their homework, but even they could not be specific about how they had been helped, although a good number felt that "TV explained current events more than their teachers" and that they preferred specific actors, newscasters, or comedians to be their teachers.

These youngsters were also significantly less in favor of censorship than were their elders; "they were less interested in optimistic coverage and more interested in a story that blamed slum life as a whole, and that described needed government action." The study found that "there was less variation by class in adolescent responses to many of our questions than in adults. Perhaps adolescents are not affected by their socio-economic position as are adults," the study conjectures, "but it is doubtful that they are the harbingers of a classless society." Instead, their attitudes may simply reflect their age; as the youngsters get older, their thinking with regard to television viewing comes close to that of the adults with whom they live and associate.

The ETS conference said that "meaningful" programs for youth were a necessity and that such programming should involve young people in the planning and production ends. The conference said further that in-school services of television stations do a poor job in so far as vocational guidance is concerned and that the educational aspect ought to receive more emphasis.

The question of television for the young is one that will continue to plague responsible public broadcasters. The commercial broadcasters, after making some attempts at programming for the young, simply abandoned their studies, labeled their new programs The *Young* Doctors or The *Young* Interns or The *Young* Rebels, and told us all they were becoming relevant to our new youth-oriented times. Public television cannot be so irresponsible. One attempt at youth programming, "The Show," originating in Hershey, Pennsylvania, was rather successful in its concept, but it was scheduled alongside such commercial blockbusters as "Bonanza" or "The F.B.I." or "Ed Sullivan" and was simply not watched. It deserved a better fate, and perhaps in the future it might get another run. As for the larger question of programming for the young, which public broadcasters obviously feel a need for, perhaps the 1970s will see abandonment of that goal and a realization that the young would prefer to be programmed for on a basis equal to that of adults. It would be an interesting program tack for public TV to take.

Many broadcasters at the conference felt that their station outlets ought to be used to some extent to further support for public education among their viewers. Floyd Christian, superintendent of Florida's Department of Education, told the public broadcasters that "One of the greatest problems facing educators today is their lack of ability to communicate with the public; to communicate with the taxpayers; and give adequate reason for the rising costs of education, the changes in the curriculum," and, he said, educators "need the help of radio and television."

Educators have long argued that television as an educational medium should do more than broadcast courses for credit. It is equipped to hold people's attention. It is equipped to change their views. It imparts impressions, and from impressions often come ideas. The use of public TV as a propaganda device for gathering support for an American institution—free public education—is an encouraging prospect. Educational broadcasting in the 1970s must not only be used as a community tool but as an educational tool as well. Mr. Siemering, with his experience at the University of Buffalo, puts these roles into perspective:

> In all too many institutions, educational broadcasting and broadcasters have occupied the same place as the Negro in American society; regarded as inherently intellectually inferior (because the medium is electronic and not print); hired for lower wages than others with comparable skills (a public relations director frequently earns more than a station manager); forced to occupy inferior crowded quarters; viewed as not fully mature (often because of reliance upon student volunteers); frequently invisible (one institution compiled a list of media resources including biology monographs and made no mention of its university radio station); and viewed as capable of offering some pleasant entertainment, but incapable of a serious academic contribution.

One can only assume that these institutions either have nothing they wish to communicate to the community or that which they wish to say can't be communicated by a mass medium. Imagine a commercial station *requesting* to go on the air with 10 watts only using the channel 25 hours a week for 36 weeks out of the year? While some commercial broadcasters have debased the content of the medium, some universities have debased the medium itself through neglect and underdevelopment. Too weak to gain popular support, too dependent upon student volunteers to prove their institutional value, these small stations are doomed to be hard half-life. These institutions fail in their responsibilities as an FCC licensee and as a public service to their communities. The FCC should establish minimum standards of power, hours of operation and staff to force these institutions to meet their responsibilities. . . . the food service must meet standards for the Board of Health; if educational broadcasting is to serve the public, it too must meet basic professional standards.

The above is a tough indictment of some sectors of public broadcasting, and one foresees great efforts to upgrade minimal service stations and improve in-school programming in the next decade. These advances are not something devoutly to be wished for by public broadcasters, but something they must address themselves to, if they are to survive.

Learning through the means of television appears to be a process in which conscious progression cannot be defined— (even those young people who say flatly that they *have* learned from TV cannot say exactly how; they just *know*), and so extended discussion of television as a medium of and for education is certainly in order, particularly how it can be utilized to greatest advantage in the future. Most sociologists agree that on a short-term basis, TV does not appear to influence people significantly or to cause them to learn radically different behavior or attitudes. But they say that on a long-range basis it is entirely possible that a cumulative effect on people can occur. What they're saying is that habitual, regular viewing can alter views, can change minds, can teach.

A recent study by Herbert J. Gans, entitled "The Uses of Television and Their Educational Implications," addresses itself to this subject. A survey of television viewers in New York which he conducted revealed that people find television "helpful, albeit in emotional rather than cognitive ways, but they certainly do not make consistent use of it as a learning instrument. Rather, as they watch, they find material that is of relevance to their daily life, and they use it when it comes up, but they do not seem to search for such material in watching television. Even the news programs, which are watched in order to provide information rather than entertainment, do not seem to be used consciously for learning purposes; people pick their newscasters less in terms of what news they present than in how they present the news, and whatever they learn seems of little importance or direct relevance to daily life, for even many regular viewers say they would not miss the programs if they could not watch them for several weeks. And if responses to a hypothetical question are any indication, there is little willingness among viewers to let themselves be influenced by a TV commentator."

Mr. Gans also found in his sampling that "Only a handful said they watch educational channels, and they tend to be viewers with above average amounts of education. This is not necessarily to say that people do not learn from TV. They may learn without being aware of learning—and thus cannot tell an interviewer what they have learned. Obviously, they are exposed to a great deal of information and opinion, yet even so, one could question whether they learn much that has direct bearing on their everyday life and their basic attitudes, or whether they learn much that they would not learn elsewhere. If TV did not exist, people would probably be less informed—both about world events and the doings of a favorite soap opera heroine—but having TV does not make them into different people."

These findings could well serve as a guide for future public broadcast programming. Perhaps educational stations ought to be evolving a multiyear audience-catching plan, wherein viewers are captured with light, entertaining programs, and once the audience is secured, the learning process could begin. But as the social scientists tell us by implication, if people become aware they are being taught at they are liable to turn off. Teaching while entertaining or maintaining escape-type attention will be a challenge for programmers in the 1970s. After all, how many "Sesame Streets" can there be around the dial?

Some, very few, public broadcasters have begun to think consciously in terms of audience numbers, but disagreements remain about how to gather them. James Day, president of the Educational Broadcasting Corporation, told me:

> We discovered more than 20 years ago how power-ful television can be in moving merchandise out of stores and into homes. Ever since then, those of us who signed on with noncommercial television have been trying to harness that power to improve the quality of life. More often than not, we have failed.
>
> I think we have failed because our approach has been worthy, dark brown and humorless. To improve the quality of life you need an audience; and to get an audi-ence you must be entertaining. I don't care how earth-shattering the issues are which public broadcasters exam-ine. If nobody is watching, nobody can care about those issues.
>
> Every so often we broadcasters launch an experiment that we herald as the single most significant communica-tions development since the invention of moveable type. Those claims are as destructive as they are absurd, and I'm happy to say that most of the programs so advertised have gone to their just reward: oblivion.

Mr. Day added that as his production of public television's "The Great American Dream Machine" was about to go on the PTV network, he intended to make "no such claim in its behalf . . . I hope that we have learned from past mistakes—our own as well as those of our commercial colleagues. I hope that the 'Machine' will have an effect on the quality of Ameri-can life because it will be entertaining, tasteful, significant, sophisticated, irresistable—and funny. In so doing it will have fulfilled its special mission and may have provided television with a long-overdue new format."

The "Dream Machine" has indeed done that. It is the most exciting television program to come along in years. It utilizes pace, short essays, commentary, political statements, man-on-the-street interviews, satire, and cartoons in order to comment on present-day America. Most television critics, including myself, thought, and think, that it is the way of television for the future. What is important is that with its format, which is—to use Mr. Day's words—"irresistible and funny," it dispenses great amounts of individual pieces of information and at the same time communicates impressions. Perhaps in the 1970s public television's network programs will embody some of the techniques of the "Dream Machine": refusal to be bound by traditional hour, half-hour, quarter-hour program segments (if a segment is three minutes long and it is artistically correct, leave it at three minutes, don't pad); and use of handheld small cameras which permits *cinéma vérité*, nonstudio photography. The latter permits coverage on location, in natural surroundings, and tends to avoid the stiltedness that comes with studio shooting.

Other men in public broadcasting—notably Messrs. Macy and Gunn—while they agree with Mr. Day's argument that audience is needed, seem determined to gather it in a different manner. Some think that there has been a deliberate effort to soft-pedal controversy on public television in the belief that the blander the programming, the broader the viewer base and thus the greater number of viewers. Commercial television since its inception has programmed for the lowest common denominator, and its annual schedules get more wretched each year. Educational television should never put itself into that programming bag, in the name of seeking wider audiences. You cannot woo audiences with intellectually inferior programs while asserting that once you have the audience you will return to uplift. Public television, if it is to be a viable, alive alternative to commercial TV must constantly experiment—must come up with other "Sesame Streets" and "Dream Machines" and "Newsrooms." It has been proven that a good concept on public TV, while publicly sneered at by commercial broadcasters, is always snapped up and copied. Public TV must be ever an innovator. "Dream Machine" showed that there was something new in entertainment that could stimulate thinking while being amusing.

Mr. Gans asks in his study what people "could and would learn from TV that they could not learn anywhere else, or that they could learn more effectively from TV?" He admits that this is a difficult question to answer because "TV may encourage learning precisely because it is not educational; people are watching to be entertained, and under such conditions, there may be less resistance to being taught than in the classroom."

Mr. Gans asserts that "people could learn something of importance from TV because of the medium's immediacy and because of the amount of time viewers spend before the screen," but he cautions, "The media cannot do the job that the school or other educational institutions have failed to do." What he says, in short, is that television cannot educate in traditional ways, but it must break new ground:

> My suggestion is that popular dramatic and comedy series can present and discuss social problems in a contemporary setting. Such programs should not deal exclusively or even predominantly with the big issues of poverty, segregation, and war that are considered society's major social problems at present, but they should deal with the everyday problems of the middle- and working-class audiences as well, the problems of family, work, home, and individual adaptation that concern most people most of the time.
>
> Such programming cannot be produced by educators, for it is clear that the moment a TV program becomes manifestly educational, it loses much of its appeal, to children and adolescents as well as adults. It must entertain as well as educate, and must therefore be created by writers and directors who know how to entertain, but can also include popular presentations of social and personal problems.

Mr. Gans goes on: This programming, he says, "must take note of the diversity of the TV audience; it must deal with problems common to all of them or to the majority most of the time, and it must present a variety of views on such problems. It cannot succeed if it presents only the professional view of a problem, because then it becomes a 'message program' and will be rejected. Rather, it must present professional as well as popular views, but it can do so in ways that will indicate the superior wisdom of the professional solution, if that solution is indeed blessed by superior wisdom. Moreover, playing off various views against each other will provide the dramatic content and conflict that a story needs in order to be popular. And when. it presents professional solutions, it must make sure that these solutions are relevant to the average audience member, and not just to the upper-middle class, well-educated person to whom most professional solutions seem most relevant today."

Perhaps first among the issues that public television ought to deal with relevantly and educationally is the place minorities—particularly the black minority—hold in this country. Despite its several black-oriented, even black-produced, programs such as "Soul!" and "Black Journal," public television's record for presenting minority views has been rather poor. Its record of acceptances of programs dealing with blacks is not as good as even that of commercial television. In 1969 the National Association of Educational Broadcasters surveyed the entire public broadcasting network at the request of the NAEB membership, some of whom believed that "educational stations not only failed to initiate local programs dealing with civil rights, but they also failed to broadcast programs about racial matters easily available to them from national network sources."

What they found was that substantial portions of the public television network were systematically turning down NET black-oriented, radical-oriented, alien-oriented offerings. The comments ranged from KLVX–Las Vegas' rejection of a "NET Journal" program entitled "Fidel" as "sugar-coated communism" and of another program on student revolutionaries because "we had our own . . . no additional instruction was necessary"; to a rejection of an "NET Playhouse" drama by WCNY–Syracuse because it did not "conform to local standards of taste."

"Black Journal" was not carried by many stations, particularly in the South. One program in the series dealing with Georgia legislator Julian Bond was not carried by WGTV in Athens, Georgia, because the station felt it would have "fanned the fire" since it commented about Governor Lester Maddox. Another "Black Journal" segment was identified as "inappropriate for university sponsorship" by the Alabama ETV network; and KETS–Conway, Arkansas, by decision of its governing commission, decided not to carry *any* of the "Black Journal" programs. KLRN in Austin, Texas, decided against carrying a network program that was devoted to minority candidates in the 1968 general elections.

This right of stations to accept or reject programs out of hand is a right they have under the Public Broadcasting Act of 1967, but the American Civil Liberties Union is going ahead with a suit which raises the question of whether the federal government doesn't have the obligation to guarantee the right of access to the media by minorities—since money appropriated by Congress for the CPB filters to these local stations. It is the ACLU's contention that to allow minority views to go unrepresented on the medium licensed—and in some cases financed—by the federal government is to deny freedom of choice to viewers in those areas. This is another question that public broadcasters will have to deal with forthrightly in this decade. Is it proper—or, in fact, legal—for broadcasters to determine what their viewers ought to see; viewers whose tax money in part subsidizes the operations of these broadcast outlets?

I believe that public broadcasters should capitalize on the fact that commercial broadcasters' records with regard to minorities have been poor; that they should open their stations and airwaves to minorities, if only to get what they want—greater audiences. I won't dwell on the obligations involved.

The NAEB Report on Program Acceptances concluded:

> Clearly, the educational station must use all the resources it can to operate effectively in the interests of the many

communities it can serve. But it is an error to think that it operates in a vacuum and can redress quickly those individual and social inequities which other institutions in the same community have not only left untended but may have perpetuated. The station alone can accomplish only so much; and a full schedule of nationally prepared programs on racial matters may do no more to advance local civil rights than re-runs of a Peggy Lee special will do to convince the resident chamber music society that it should change its repertoire.

True, as far as it goes. But the programs might do some good, might educate, if they were simply shown. To adhere to the above statement and to lean on it when a broadcaster declines to televise certain programs is to avoid responsibility. Indeed one challenge for the 70s will be, will local stations cease being narrowly parochial and open their signals to all the people?

Their performance in the past with regard to programs such as those mentioned contrasts markedly with local broadcasters' efforts in other areas of local coverage. Often they have done what commercial broadcasters will not and cannot do. In Connecticut the state public network provides regular coverage of the state legislature; as does KTPS in Tacoma, Washington. WJCT in Jacksonville, Florida, WETA in Washington, D.C., and WHYY in Philadelphia regularly cover city council and school board meetings. The Nebraska State ETV Network took viewers on tours of the State Museum, the Governor's Mansion, and the State Capitol and broadcast concerts of the Omaha Symphony Orchestra.

KRMA in Denver has become a champion of the western environment and WQED in Pittsburgh ran a saturation anti-drug series of programs. KSJN in Minneapolis–St. Paul and KSJR in Collegeville, Minnesota, have a 17-hour "Radio Talking Book" for the blind; KETS in Little Rock produced a four-part TV record of "The Folk Music of the Ozarks"; the Vermont Public TV Network produced "The Sights and Sounds of Vermont"; and WMVS in Milwaukee broadcast four television programs in conjunction with the opening of the city's Performing Arts Center and covered the Wisconsin State Fair.

The South Carolina public TV network regularly broadcasts "Job Man Caravan" in efforts to reduce unemployment. WMPB in Baltimore covered live the twenty-eight hours of hearings in that city of the U.S. Commission on Civil Rights. WHRS in Lake Worth, Florida, carries a daily program for migrant workers. KPFK in Los Angeles operates a Watts Bureau from which news of that black community is broadcast. WBFO in Buffalo operates an inner-city satellite studio.

WUSF in Tampa produced its own series of consumer education programs; WITF in Hershey, Pennsylvania, gave elderly viewers a weekly series, "The Time of Our Lives"; WKAR in East Lansing, Michigan, directed "Variedades en Español" to its Mexican-American community. The Maine ETV network produced a three-part series featuring Down East storyteller Marshall Dodge. Also reflecting regional interests was a WYES (New Orleans) special on "Cajun Ways." KEBS in San Diego presented a four-part "Science and Society" series.

The average public television station produces about 24 percent of the programs it airs, compared to about 16 percent for the average commercial station. It is to be hoped that this percentage will increase in the 1970s, although there is the fear that as the PBS network sends more programs down the line, local stations—like their commercial counterparts—will become lazy.

One weakness that public broadcasting will have to overcome in the coming years is its lack of VHF stations. Because both the widely watched VHF and the rarely watched UHF stations are allocated by the Federal Communications Commission, it may be necessary for public television to make its case for equality as a network to the FCC and request more VHF outlets. In Washington, for example, where both CPB and PBS are located, station WETA—soon to be the seat of a new television news service—is UHF and its viewing audience is negligible. The same circumstances prevail in Los Angeles, Detroit, and Cincinnati.

As of January 4, 1971, there were 884 television stations in the United States. Of these 682 were commercial, 202 noncommercial. More important, of the 590 VHF licensed stations, 503 were commercial and only 87 noncommercial; whereas there were 179 commercial UHFs and 115 noncommercial UHFs. In other words, only about 40 percent of public noncommercial stations had allocations on the more widely watched VHF frequencies, but commercial stations had about 85 percent of their licenses assigned to VHF frequencies. The numbers point to the patent unfairness of the station allocations by the FCC and give public television goals to shoot at if it is to emerge in the 1970s as a true alternative viewing source for American viewers. It is a fact, for example, that in most black inner-city ghettos, the viewing audiences do not have UHF-equipped television sets and are therefore deprived very often of public television's jewel, "Sesame Street," which is aimed at poor preschoolers. Fred Friendly, who wishes to see public television with a news interconnection—an alternative to commercial network news offerings, told me that "public television without VHF outlets is a farce."

Mr. Friendly, in a March 1971 address at the University of Michigan, made another proposal which could alter the face not only of public television in the next decade, but also of TV journalism generally. He proposed creation of an electronic television news service with public television a joint partner with the American Broadcasting Company, the Columbia Broadcasting System and the National Broadcasting Company news organizations. He suggested that for scheduled news events—such as cabinet-level statements, VIP airport departures, predictable news conferences—duplicate coverage by all four networks be eliminated; one camera crew could be assigned from a central dispatching station, and videotape of the conference or event be sent along to the individual networks. He argued that such coverage would not kill journalistic initiative, because networks could still send their own reporters to the events, but rather would "free the correspondents and cameramen for those enterprise assignments which are the very essence of comprehensive, truly competitive journalism.

"It would free journalists to report news rather than just cover events whose agenda is so often set by publicists. It would make them explainers of complicated issues rather than what a veteran Washington news hand calls journalist stenographers."

Mr. Friendly tentatively dubbed his proposal the Broadcast News Service or Television News Service and said the method of distribution of covered material could be by microwave or satellite circuits where feeds could come into videotape recorders for use on evening news programs. "Preliminary judgment suggests," he said, "that a consortium of users, that is, the major commercial networks, public television and those independent stations which desire to fulfill their public service requirements, possibly together with United Press International-Television News, and Viz News, the British Commonwealth News Service which has an exchange agreement with NBC News, could form a non-profit organization similar to the Associated Press or the News Election Service."

Duplication of crews, film stock, processing equipment, and delivery mechanisms would be eliminated under his proposal, Mr. Friendly said, and he urged: "The opportunity now for an electronic news service exists because the technology is right; because there is a certain restiveness among some serious observers about the price we may be paying for overkill in the name of front page competition, and because the broadcast industry, no longer the fat cat it once was, cannot afford to waste either its resources or time. Most of all, an under-informed America cannot survive. In an age of satellites and wired cities, technology may change television as much as television changed radio."

The reaction among public broadcasters was positive, but for the most part shortsighted. They saw themselves reaping the benefits of network-style news coverage simply by buying a videotape receiver. Among commercial broadcasters there seemed to be cautious endorsement of the concept but some reluctance to turn over to other editing teams what they wished to cut and present themselves. Whether public television will join with commercial television in this venture is another question it will answer in this decade, for it is certainly true that television news—watched by millions of Americans

41

as their only source of information—is generally inadequate; and on public television it is barely minimal.

Public television's record in the field of documentary programming has been enviable. The best documentaries in recent years, the most controversial and the most independent, have been on public TV. But in day-to-day news coverage and presentation the country's PTV stations are literally years out of step with commercial television. In many instances it is because small public stations, lacking funds to buy sophisticated sound, film, and tape equipment, often rent studio facilities. In New York City, for example, the nightly newscast on the public television Channel 13 was until recently simply a radio broadcast accompanied by slides and some unimaginative graphics. Viewers could hardly be expected to turn away from the slickly produced commercial news programs for such fare as this. And what generally has passed for analysis of news has been three or four people sitting in chairs around a cocktail table ponderously opining. It was dull and nobody watched.

The lack was particularly noticeable in political coverage. Public television had not the crews to cover candidates on a daily basis and often chose to read terse wire service accounts in lieu of in-depth coverage. Public television's performance in this area has been studied and reported on at great length in "Public Television and Political Broadcasting: A Matter of Responsibility" by Harold Mendelsohn, chairman of the Department of Mass Communications at the University of Denver, and Melvyn M. Muchnik, an instructor in the department. The study is highly critical of public broadcasting as a political educator—a function it should perform:

> It has been customary for public broadcasting to suggest that it is free from the economic political pressure and influences that allegedly bedevil the independence of commercial broadcasting. The implication here is that public broadcasters need not fear the economic/political wrath of advertisers or consumers in presenting so-called unpopular fare. Further, it is usual for public broadcasters, in attempting to gain public support, to point out

their freedom from having to address themselves to specific air-time limitations. Nor do public broadcasters appear to show unusual concern relating to "in-depth" programming; scheduling lengthy time blocks for programs of particular public interest; or, for that matter, audience ratings. . . .

According to its own rhetoric, public broadcasting poses a serious "alternative" to commercial broadcasting in the political arena. Still, for reasons that are not readily manifest, public broadcasting has shown considerable reluctance to move into political education—most noticeably during election campaigns. Curious as well has been the silence of the critics in pointing out the responsibilities of the sacred-cow public broadcasting sector in political broadcasting.

The University of Denver team asks "is there not a tendency among public broadcasters to soothe their own consciences by ducking behind the convenient screen of 'lack of budget' when they too fail to serve the public adequately during periods of high political crises; that is, during election campaigns?" and answers by citing responses to their survey which has public broadcasters admitting that they steer clear of political endorsement or controversy; that their personnel are inadequate for sophisticated coverage; and that they do not wish to duplicate commercial TV coverage. "This no doubt will come as a somewhat shocking surprise to the millions of taxpayers and voluntary contributors who have been led to support PTV on the basis of a reverse argument."

The study concludes, "How long can public television fail to address itself seriously to this issue, perhaps the most consequential issue it must resolve before it can legitimately lay claim to massive public confidence and support?"

How long indeed! This glaring gap in public television's performance still exists and it will not be solved by scheduling "debates" devoted to presentation of "all sides of all issues." Points of view are to be expected of a medium which contends it is free of political pressure. Disregard of the twinges of commercial sponsors should be expected of a medium that

43

contends it is free of economic pressure. But some observers contend that in its haste to become a network on par with the existing big three, public television has avoided controversy so that there will be no waves from Congress which could interfere with financing appropriations, and so that commercial organizations which could underwrite future projects would not be offended.

If public television is to be truly representative of the public, broadcasters should not care what a certain congressman or retail chain-store owner thinks about programming. The broadcaster should listen to what they have to say, and if he feels there is merit in their contentions, then he ought to provide them with forums. But they should not be permitted veto power—explicit or implicit—as maybe the case with many public broadcasting outlets today.

If public TV is to be significant in the next decade, it must be intellectually courageous and beholden to none. This can be done in several ways. Adequate permanent long-term financing can provide a measure of freedom from pressure, and laws can mandate noninterference. But courage must come from within.

It will take courage to break new programming ground. It will take courage to resist economic and political considerations and devote one's self to meaningful controversy. It will take a good deal of courage for public broadcasters to ask money from sources which they might have to criticize. It will take courage to ensure access to public broadcasting by the community at large and by the minorities within that community. It will take courage and vision to use the television as a tool of political and social education. It will take courage to cover news as it should be covered. Without this courage public broadcasting in the 1970s will have failed its early promise.

What is needed to shape the future of public television is the daring of the past combined with the technology of the present. The technology is there, but without the daring, public television will continue to remain the stepchild of commercial television; the plaything for those who want to dabble electronically. But mostly it will remain unwatched.

Filmography

Television is so evanescent a medium. It is there, it captures the attention, it involves, and then quickly it is gone. Television is not like a book, to which one can return repeatedly to enjoy again a chapter, a passage, a sentence, a word perhaps. How many of us have said to friends, "You should have seen this or that program last night," and then gone on to rhapsodize over it. Later we ourselves may wish to see it again and share it with others, but knowing that except for the occasional rerun, what was seen is gone. It is television's strength that it can involve one so completely and intimately, and it is its weakness that it cuts off that involvement at the stroke of an hour.

Commercial television tends to repeat most of the programs and events it schedules, but with relatively few exceptions its products are less than memorable and not worth repetition except as vehicles for carrying advertising. Public television's track records over the years have been somewhat better, with more programs worth seeing again. But its distribution facilities, particularly on a network level, have been inadequate.

In the last few years efforts have been made to make up for that lack. Realizing that it did not have the communications linkups that the commercial networks have, public television has had to rely principally on mail distribution. It filmed and taped programs, broadcast them, and then if other stations wanted the programs they had to obtain them through the stations, who had not the time to set up cataloged film libraries. It was cumbersome and resulted in missed mailings, in frustrations for programmers.

Under the sponsorship of public television's membership group, the National Association of Educational Broadcasters, a program service was established on the grounds of Indiana University in Bloomington. It grew, became diversified and sophisticated, and today is the major supplier of public television films and tapes in the country. Stations from all over the country send their master films and tapes to Bloomington for redistribution.

Under the general supervision of the university's Audio-Visual Center are: Public Broadcasting Service Library Service (formerly the Educational Television Stations Program Service), P.O. Box 1430, 512 17th St., Bloomington 47401; National Instructional Television Center, Box A, Bloomington 47401; and National Educational Television Programs, Audio-Visual Center, Indiana University, Bloomington 47401. NET taped programs for cable television use are also available from NET CATV Projects, 10 Columbus Circle, New York City 10219. A selected list of films available from the Public Broadcasting Service Library Service and the Audio-Visual Center at Indiana University follows:

Albert Herring   120 min. B & W. Rental $50.

A full-length studio production of Benjamin Britten's opera, restaged for television and performed by the Indiana University Opera Theater Company and Orchestra.

America: On the Edge of Abundance   59 min. B & W. Rental $12.

Explores the far-reaching economic and social consequences of the increasingly automated and computer-oriented society in the United States as viewed by British Television. (NET)

Anatomy of Violence   30 min. B & W. Purchase $125; rental $6.95.

Presents several speeches on the relationship of violence to social reform. The speakers are part of a two-week Congress on the Dialectics of Liberation held in London. Among those who appear are Professor Herbert Marcuse, Paul Goodman, Stokely Carmichael, and Allen Ginsberg. In addition two social scientists evaluate the conference in a discussion with David Prowitt, National Educational Television. (NET)

Angry Negro   30 min. B & W. Purchase $125; rental $6.75.

In this film the leaders of debate within the Negro community express varied opinions about the way the Negro should go in his search for equality. Interviews are presented with: Elijah Muhammad of the Black Muslims; Daniel Watts, editor of *Liberator* magazine; Jimmy Garret from the Congress of Racial Equality; Fannie Lou Hamer, one of the founders of the Mississippi Freedom Democratic Party; Julian

Bond of the Student Non-Violent Coordinating Committee; John Lewis, co-founder of SNCC; and Andrew Young of the Southern Christian Leadership Conference. (NET)

Appalachia: Rich Land Poor People   59 min. B & W. Purchase $240; rental $13.

The land is rich with coal, yet its residents are denied adequate food, housing, and medical care. This, the Appalachian region, was the nation's first designated poverty area. This film focuses upon Eastern Kentucky where mechanization of the mines is replacing people and jobs and a lack of education and other working skills makes these residents prisoners of the land, as seen by a discerning interview with a local family. (NET)

Artists: Claes Oldenburg   30 min. B & W. Purchase $125; rental $6.75.

An introduction to Claes Oldenburg, his studio, his personality, his reasons for doing what he does, and his works. Oldenburg is shown working and preparing for a major exhibition of his new works. Many examples of his works are shown. (NET)

Artists: Jack Tworkov   30 min. B & W. Purchase $125; rental $6.75.

An introduction to the abstract expressionism of Jack Tworkov and his thoughts about the meaningfulness of his work, along with a description of the events that led him to become an artist. (NET)

Artists: Robert Rauschenberg   30 min. B & W. Purchase $125; rental $6.75.

At the peak of his greatest fame as a painter Robert Rauschenberg stopped painting altogether; in this film Rauschenberg discusses his reasons for ceasing to paint and explains where he now hopes to go in his art. (NET)

Audubon   58 min. Color. Rental $18.

A documentary which traces the travels of John J. Audubon (1785–1851) throughout Europe and North America. Although Audubon named, classified, and wrote about birds, he is probably best known as an artist. The minute detail he portrayed as he painted birds in a natural setting can be seen in film scenes taken from his most famous book, *The Birds of America*. (NET)

Banquet of Life   60 min. B & W. Rental $12.

An essay which investigates the various sources of food from hunting and fishing to automated farms in order to document man's efforts to feed his ever increasing numbers. The results of the investigation indicate that growing more food will not avert ultimate famine. (NET)

Battered Child   58 min. B & W. Purchase $240; rental $13.

A documentary study of child abuse based on the book *The Battered Child* by Drs. C. Henry Kempe and Roy E. Helfer. These doctors have created a team consisting of psychiatrists, pediatricians, and social workers to study the causes of physical child abuse and to treat children affected mentally. The team is shown at the University of Colorado Medical Center working with actual cases. (NET)

Beaux-Arts String Quartet   60 min. Color. Rental $25.

A studio concert performed by the Beaux-Arts String Quartet of New York. The program is devoted to two works— Beethoven's Quartet in F Major, no. 1, opus 18 and the Ravel Quartet in F Major.

Black G.I.   55 min. B & W. Purchase $265; rental $12.25.

The black soldier is discriminated against both on and off military bases. This film, produced on location, includes interviews with black servicemen and Pentagon officials. Originally produced for "Black Journal." (NET)

Bomb   30 min. B & W. Purchase $125; rental $6.75.

This film presents a brief history of the development of nuclear bombs and a discussion of the problems caused by plutonium which is a by-product of nuclear reactors. (NET)

The Brandywine Tradition   30 min. Color. Rental $12.50.

A half-hour documentary on illustrator Newell Convers

Wyeth's philosophy and work which sparked two succeeding generations of Wyeths.

Chain of Life 30 min. Color. Purchase $315; rental $11.50.

Man, as an end link in "the chain of life," is limiting his own survival when he destroys other links of that chain. A healthy environment is as essential to the survival of plants and animals as to man, who eventually must consume those plants and animals. (NET)

Chicano 30 min. Color. Rental $12.50.

A pictorial diary of Chicano life as seen through the eyes of San Diego's young Mexican-Americans.

Cities and the Poor—Part 1 60 min. B & W. Purchase $200; rental $12.

An introduction to the problems of the urban poor in the United States which explores who the poor are, where they are, and the reasons for their dilemma. (NET)

Cities and the Poor—Part 2 60 min. B & W. Purchase $200; rental $12.

The second of two films on poverty in the cities explores the rise of militant groups among the urban poor. Neighborhood organizations in Chicago and Los Angeles are studied as typical examples. (NET)

Cities—The Rise of New Towns 60 min. B & W. Purchase $200; rental $12.

The building of totally planned communities is explained and Reston, Virginia; Foster City and Irvine, California; Columbia, Maryland; Tapiola, Finland; and Vallingby, Sweden, are shown. The economic, sociological, and governmental implications of this movement is discussed. (NET)

Civil Disorder: The Kerner Report—Parts 1 & 2 56 min. B & W. Purchase $240; rental $11.75.
Part 1

Several examples of what the Kerner Report called "the polarization of the American community" are presented. These include a statement of the goals of the Negro revolution by a Negro militant and scenes of white housewives learning to shoot to kill.

Part 2

A continuation of part 1 presents examples of efforts to relieve Negro underemployment and a review of the Kerner Report as a social document by author James Baldwin. (PBL/NET)

Civil Disorder: The Kerner Report—Part 3 24 min. B & W. Purchase $150; rental $6.

Three prominent Negroes analyze the Kerner Report in terms of whether or not they believe anything will be done in response to the report and if there still is time. Charles V. Hamilton, Bayard Rustin, and Kenneth Clark participate in a panel discussion. (PBL/NET)

Civil Disorder: The Kerner Report—Parts 1, 2, & 3 80 min. B & W. Purchase $300; rental $17.75.

This three-part film may be ordered as one film for the above prices.

Classical Ballet 29 min. B & W. Purchase $125; rental $6.75.

Presents a brief history of classical ballet and demonstrates the essential positions and steps every student must learn. Maria Tallchief and Andrew Eglevsky perform the pas de deux from *Swan Lake* and *Sylvia*.

Color Us Black 60 min. B & W. Purchase $240; rental $13.

The black man's struggle for his own identity over and above the "norm" is covered from the point of view of Negro students at predominantly black Howard University in Washington, D.C. The four-day takeover of the administration building by students seeking to overcome what they call the "irrelevant" curriculum at the university is shown, including the successful ending of the rebellion. (NET)

Community 59 min. B & W. Purchase $200; rental $12.

Evaluates the cultural, educational, religious, and physical aspects of America's cities and towns. Focuses on the small

New England fishing community of Provincetown and compares it with San Jose, California, a booming western community in the midst of accelerated growth. (NET)

Confrontation: Dialogue in Black and White 35 min. B & W. Rental $15.

At the end of a tense summer in Chicago, one hundred citizens were invited to a studio of station WTTW to confront each other with their views on the racial situation. The debate is preceded by presentation of a film produced and directed by a Negro militant. Then militants and moderates in the Negro and white audience are shown as they freely express themselves. (PBL/NET)

Control of a Crisis 30 min. B & W. Purchase $125; rental $6.75.

An analysis of the Berlin crisis of 1961 and the Cuban missile crisis of 1962. (NET)

Culture Explosion 60 min. B & W. Rental $12.

Culture Explosion samples the types of art which have increased in popularity with the general public in Canada, England, and the United States and presents interviews with artists and critics to gain insight into the nature of this growth. Symphonic music, classic paintings, "op" art, "pop" art, underground movies, cinema, poetry, and opera are examined in terms of which segments of the public are supporting them and the reasons behind such support. (NET)

Dance: Four Pioneers 30 min. B & W. Purchase $125; rental $6.75.

This film introduces the four major choreographers (Martha Graham, Doris Humphrey, Charles Weidman, and Hanya Holm) who revolted against the conventions of ballet to produce American modern dance. (NET)

Daniel Watts 30 min. B & W. Purchase $150; rental $7.25.

Daniel H. Watts, editor of the *Liberator* and one of the leading theoreticians of Black Nationalism in America, is interviewed by Donald Fouser. (NET)

DeGrazia   30 min. Color. Rental $12.50.

Ted DeGrazia, an Arizona artist of many styles, is profiled on this award-winning program filmed on location.

Diary of a Student Revolution   59 min. B & W. Purchase $240; rental $13.

On-campus industrial recruiting of students at the University of Connecticut resulted in confrontation between student activities and the university president. NET used two camera crews working independently to simultaneously show the philosophies and strategies of both sides during the conflict. (NET)

Entrepreneur: Part 1   29 min. B & W. Purchase $125; rental $6.75.

Presents three representatives of entrepreneurial activity who are questioned about their businesses: James S. McDonnell, President, McDonnell Aircraft Corporation; Joseph Sunnen, President, Sunnen Products Company; and Sam Wolff, President, Wolff-Taber Shoe Company.

Entrepreneur: Part 2   29 min. B & W. Purchase $125; rental $6.75.

Continues the examination of the entrepreneur from *The Entrepreneur: Part 1*.

Essay on William Blake   52 min. Color. Purchase $550; rental $19.

The life of William Blake (1757–1827) is acted out in this drama of a man alternately regarded as a heretic, a religious poet, an idealist, and a mad man while living. (NET)

Fasten Your Seatbelts—A Report on Airline Safety   60 min. B & W. Purchase $240; rental $13.

An examination of airline safety and problems associated with it. (NET)

Fence around the Amish   30 min. B & W. Rental $12.50.

A sensitive and penetrating documentary of the Amish way of life in the United States, told in paint and charcoal by Pennsylvania artist Florence Taylor.

Frontier American   29 min. B & W. Purchase $125; rental $6.75.

Visits Fence Lake, New Mexico, to discover something of the spirit which drew Americans across the continent. Homesteaders of Fence Lake explain what made them leave their old homes to go to the frontier.

Gandhi's India   58 min. B & W. Rental $13.50.

The life of Mohandas Karamehand (Mahatma) Gandhi (1869–1948) and his influence on present-day India are examined in this film.

Goodbye and Good Luck   30 min. B & W. Purchase $150; rental $7.25.

A documentary of an encounter between advocates of "Black Power" and a Negro Vietnam veteran. (PBL/NET)

God Is Dead   30 min. B & W. Purchase $125; rental $6.75.

A series of filmed interviews both pro and con on the controversial theology of Dr. Thomas J. J. Altizer who has advanced the "God is dead" idea. (NET)

Grassroots   34 min. B & W. Purchase $125; rental $6.75.

Presents a camera exploration of Princeton, Kentucky. Combines commentary by the inhabitants, local background music, and a detailed photographic examination of people, buildings, animals, and scenery that make up this town.

Great Label Mystery   60 min. B & W. Purchase $200; rental $12.

This film examines food, drug, and domestic packaging practices and the controversy that has risen from the "truth in packaging" legislation introduced by U.S. Senator Philip A. Hart (D-Michigan). (NET)

Gwendolyn Brooks   30 min. B & W. Purchase $125; rental $6.75.

An introduction to the poetry and personality of Gwendolyn Brooks and the Chicago environment which provided the sources for most of her materials. (NET)

Hard Times in the Country 58 min. Color: Purchase $550; rental $20.50. B & W: Purchase $265; rental $13.50.

The effects of the increasing consolidation of the food industry upon consumers and farmers are examined in this film. (NET)

Henry Roth 30 min. B & W. Purchase $125; rental $6.75.

A series of interviews between Henry Roth, author of *Call It Sleep*, and John Williams, another American novelist, during which Roth discusses his first novel and its effect upon his life. (NET)

Heritage of the Negro 30 min. B & W. Purchase $125; rental $6.75.

Explores the heritage of the Negro by examining the civilization and achievements of ancient Africa and their significance to the American Negro today. (NET)

Homosexuality in Men and Women 60 min. B & W. Rental $12.

This film provides an insight into homosexual conditions as reporter Bryan Magee interviews homosexuals and lesbians in England and Holland. (NET)

Iron Horse 30 min. B & W. Purchase $125; rental $6.75.

Recalls the era of massive railroad construction west of the Mississippi and cites the growth of two railroad companies—the California-chartered Central Pacific and the federal-chartered Union Pacific. (NET)

Irving Howe 30 min. B & W. Purchase $150; rental $7.25.

Donald Fouser discusses democratic socialism with Irving Howe, editor of *Dissent* magazine and professor of English at Hunter College, New York City. (NET)

Journalism—Mirror, Mirror on the World? 52 min. B & W. Purchase $240; rental $11.75.

An analysis of news reporting which compares coverage of a peace demonstration by the Public Broadcast Laboratory, NBC's David Brinkley, the *Washington Post*, United Press International, and the *New York Times*. (PBL/NET)

Last Reflections on a War   44 min. B & W. Purchase $210; rental $10.

Following an introduction by his widow, the critical comments and views of Asian scholar and war correspondent Bernard B. Fall are presented along with combat scenes from South Vietnam. (PBL/NET)

Lay My Burden Down   60 min. B & W. Purchase $200; rental $12.

Documents the economic and educational plight of the Negro tenant farmers of the southern United States whose average earnings are less than $1,000 a year. (NET)

Margaret Mead's New Guinea Journal   90 min. Color. Purchase $510; rental $23. B & W. Purchase $325; rental $17.

Margaret Mead, famous anthropologist, looks at change in the village of Perio on Manus, one of the Admiralty Islands in Australian Trust Territory of New Guinea. Between Dr. Mead's first two visits to the village in 1928 and 1953, Perio moved from the Stone Age into the twentieth century.

Martin Luther King: The Man and the March   83 min. B & W. Purchase $325; rental $17.

A documentary which records the history of the late Dr. Martin Luther King's "Poor People's March."

Mexican Americans—The Invisible Minority   38 min. Color. Purchase $300; rental $12.50. B & W. Purchase $180; rental $9.25.

A view of five million Mexican-Americans, our second largest and fastest growing ethnic minority, struggling for an identity within the protest movement. (PBL/NET)

Mr. Smith and Other Nonsense   30 min. Color. Rental $12.50.

William Jay Smith, poetry consultant to the Library of Congress, captures the whimsy and humor of children's poetry through his readings enhanced by imaginative, animated art work and special effects.

55

Mr. Thoreau Takes a Trip: A Week on the Concord & the Merrimack   30 min. B & W. Rental $12.50.

A program recreating the impression of Henry David Thoreau on a trip he took with his brother in August 1839 and recorded in his book, *A Week on the Concord and Merrimack Rivers.*

Music Makers of the Blue Ridge   48 min. B & W. Purchase $175; rental $10.25.

This film provides the viewer with a generous sample of the traditional melodies, verses, and dances which are indigenous to the Blue Ridge Mountains of western North Carolina. (NET)

Navaho: Part 1   29 min. B & W. Purchase $125; rental $6.75.

Presents a visit to a Navaho reservation to discover the values held by this indigenous community.

Navaho: Part 2   29 min. B & W. Purchase $125; rental $6.75.

Presents a visit to Windrock, Arizona, to interview members of the Navaho Tribes Council. Discusses the problems of working within the tribal organizational patterns and of the continuing force of tradition.

None of My Business   32 min. B & W. Purchase $180; rental $8.

Examines the widespread—often fallacious—notions about welfare recipients. (PBL/NET)

Novel: 1914–1942 The Loss of Innocence   30 min. B & W. Purchase $125; rental $6.75.

This film explores the themes of the major works of Ernest Hemingway, John Dos Passos, Sherwood Anderson, John Steinbeck, Thomas Wolfe, F. Scott Fitzgerald, James T. Farrell and examines the way in which each author drew on the experiences of people from different geographical regions of America for material to include in his novel. (NET)

Novel: Vladimir Nabokov   29 min. B & W. Purchase $125; rental $6.75.

This film presents several interviews with Vladimir Nabokov during which he gives us his opinion of what the literary masterpieces of this country are and tells what he thinks of American writing. (NET)

Old Age—Out of Sight Out of Mind   60 min. B & W. Purchase $200; rental $12.

A documentary on the institutions and rehabilitation programs available for the aged. Included are segments from the U.S. Senate's subcommittee investigation of nursing homes during which nursing home proprietors are interviewed by Senators Kennedy of Massachusetts and Neuberger of Oregon. (NET)

Of Broccoli and Pelicans and Celery and Seals   30 min. Color. Purchase $315; rental $11.50.

A survey of pesticides spraying on the Oxnard Plain in California which is washed to sea where they are contaminating fishes which are, in turn, eaten by birds, seals, and man. Tragic scenes show pelican eggs breaking because of DDT's interference with calcium production.

Past, Present and Future   30 min. B & W. Purchase $125; rental $6.75.

A discussion of the history of radicalism in this country and its possible effects upon the society of the future. (NET)

Poetry: In Search of Hart Crane   90 min. B & W. Purchase $275; rental $16.

The biography of poet Hart Crane is revealed as the camera looks on while his biographer searches Crane's books, papers, and other memorabilia for clues to the artist's personality and conducts interviews with friends and associates of Crane. (NET)

Poetry: Richard Wilbur and Robert Lowell   30 min. B & W. Purchase $125; rental $6.75.

A filmed interview with Richard Wilbur during which he explains his interest in the formal means of poetic expression and reads from several of his recent poems, and an interview with Robert Lowell in which he describes the origin of the ideas behind several of his poems before reading them. (NET)

57

Point of View 29 min. B & W Purchase $150; rental $7.25.

Shows Ansel Adams as he photographs an old house and its inhabitants. Explains his "point of view" as he photographs from many different perspectives.

Poor Pay More 60 min. B & W. Purchase $200; rental $12.

This film provides a close look at the special hardships faced by the poor in the area of consumer purchasing.

Prairie Killers 30 min. Color. Purchase $315; rental $11.50.

Ranchers displeased that coyotes may kill a few sheep and that prairie dogs eat grass, change the ecological balance by destroying these animals and a vital part of the chain of life on the plains.

Prudhoe Bay—or Bust! 30 min. Color. Purchase $315; rental $11.50.

A look at the monetary interests and ecological and conservation interests at odds over the issue of building 800 miles of hot oil pipeline through the Arctic Tundra in Alaska. (NET)

Rank and File 15 min. B & W. Purchase $110; rental $5.25.

In the New York local of the Transport Workers Union, blacks and Puerto Ricans are fighting to form their own union in order to counter the discrimination they find in the present union. Originally produced for "Black Journal." (NET)

Right of Privacy 59 min. B & W. Purchase $240; rental $13.

A report on the governmental and business activities which pose a threat to individual privacy today and the possible elimination of all privacy should the proposed National Data Center be established. (NET)

Right Takes Over 30 min. B & W. Purchase $125; rental $6.75.

A report featuring former citizens of Centralia, Missouri, who tell of the dominance of right-wing political interests in this basically one-industry town.

Roots of Hillbilly Music   29 min. B & W. Purchase $125; rental $6.75.

Presents considerable historical background and numerous examples of hillbilly music. Includes information about the music and its past and present performers.

Santa Barbara—Everybody's Mistake   30 min. Color. Purchase $315; rental $11.50.

Santa Barbara—Everybody's Mistake examines controversies behind the two-million-gallon California off-shore leak in 1969. (NET)

Slow Death of Desert Water   30 min. Color. Purchase $315; rental $11.50.

A look at Pyramid Lake, in Nevada, which is drying up because of man's interference with nature. (NET)

Television: A Political Machine?   14 min. B & W. Purchase $100; rental $5.

The use of television by the candidates running in the 1968 Indiana presidential primary is the occasion for this examination of how politics is affected by a mass medium. Attention is given to the candidate as a television personality, the role of newscasts, and the character of paid political announcements. (PBL/NET)

This Is Rodeo   30 min. Color. Rental $12.50.

This Is Rodeo captures all the color, fascination, and excitement of the western rodeo—from bulldogging to chuck wagon racing; includes all the fast-paced action of the rodeo circuits of Colorado, New Mexico, and Wyoming.

This Question of Violence   59 min. B & W. Purchase $240; rental $13.

An in-depth report on the historical, social, and psychological factors that seem to underlie violence in modern life. (NET)

To Calm a Troubled Campus   32 min. B & W. Purchase $180; rental $8.

A nonviolent demonstration against military research and university expansion into a neighboring ghetto at the University of Pennsylvania results in a negotiated settlement which showed the progressiveness of both the university and the students. (NET)

Trial: The City and County of Denver Versus Lauren R. Watson Series.

This is the first television broadcast of an actual courtroom trial. The defendant, Lauren R. Watson, is former minister of defense of the Black Panther Party in Denver, Colorado. He charges continuous police harassment. Watson is being defended by Leonard Davies who firmly believes in the American system of law but doubts that it is possible for a black man to get a fair trial without a jury of peers. The prosecution is led by Wright J. Morgan who believes that racial composition of the jury is unimportant. The judge, the Hon. Zita Weinshienk, is Denver's first and only woman judge. At the end of each day of the trial James Vorenberg of the Harvard University Law School discusses the legal questions concerning the case. (NET)

a *Trial: The First Day*   90 min. B & W. Purchase $360; rental $18.

A jury of six are selected to try defendant Lauren R. Watson for interfering with a police officer and resisting arrest.

b *Trial: The Second Day*   90 min. B & W. Purchase $360; rental $18.

The prosecution presents its case against Lauren Watson in this first day of the actual trial.

c *Trial: The Third Day*   90 min. B & W. Purchase $360; rental $18.

The prosecution rests its case and the defense, after making a motion for a judgment of acquittal, presents its witnesses.

d *Trial: The Fourth and Final Day*   90 min. B & W. Purchase 360; rental $18.

In this final day of *Trial* both sides rest their cases after closing arguments. Instructions are given to the jury which then spends two hours deliberating on the verdict. During jury deliberation interviews are conducted with the judge, the arresting officer, both attorneys, and the defendant. After the verdict is returned, interviews are conducted with some of the jury members to determine why they voted as they did.

Tribute to Malcolm X 15 min. B & W. Purchase $100; rental $5.

The influence of Malcolm X upon the present black liberation movement is reported on in this film. (NET)

Triumph of Christy Brown 60 min. B & W. Rental $54.

This document, filmed in Dublin, Ireland, traces the life of Christy Brown, author of *My Left Foot* and *Down All the Days*. Brown has been afflicted with cerebral palsy since birth and has had full use of only his left foot with which to do his painting and writing.

Troubled Cities 60 min. B & W. Purchase $200; rental $12.

A documentary which probes the attempts which are being made to solve the problems which have been brought about by the urban population explosion. (NET)

Voices from the Right 30 min. B & W. Purchase $125; rental $6.75.

This film presents some of the people—both those well known and some who are obscure—who speak for the radical right. These people explain what the radical right stands for and opposes. (NET)

War Plans 30 min. B & W. Purchase $125; rental $6.75.

A review of the conflict between the plan to prevent war by threatening massive nuclear retaliation to any nation that begins a war and the plan to maintain flexibility so that these weapons might be used only to whatever extent is necessary to show an enemy that to continue hostilities means disaster. The advantages and disadvantages of both strategies are discussed by international leaders. (NET)

Warren Years: The Great Decisions 24 min. B & W. Purchase $150; rental $6.

Major Supreme Court rulings in the areas of school desegregation and civil rights, reapportionment, and criminal procedure are examined in light of the consequences of the decisions. (NET)

Water Is So Clear That a Blind Man Could See 30 min. Color. Purchase $315; rental $11.50.

An examination of New Mexico's Taos Indians and their ancestral homeland.

Welfare Revolt 60 min. B & W. Purchase $240; rental $13.

A report documenting the complaints of welfare recipients and their attempts to change the system by organizing local unions. (NET)

What's New on the Left? 30 min. B & W. Purchase $125; rental $6.75.

Speakers for the organizations now collectively known as the "new Left" give their views of what the "new Left" stands for. (NET)

Who Invited Us? 60 min. B & W. Purchase $265; rental $13.50.

This documentary reviews the history of the United States military intervention beginning with the takeover of the Philippines and continuing through the Viet Nam war. (NET)

Who Speaks for Man? 56 min. Color. Purchase $420; rental $16.50. B & W. Purchase $240; rental $11.75.

The United Nations, originally thought to be the articulated conscience of the world and a hope for world brotherhood, is critically examined in this film. (NET)

Who Teaches Them? 30 min. B & W. Purchase $125; rental $6.75.

Schools in America with a radically Left or radically Right orientation are compared, revealing something about their teachings and interviewing some of their teachers. (NET)

Whole World Is Watching   55 min. B & W. Purchase $240; rental $11.75.

Television reporters including David Brinkley and Walter Cronkite and critics such as Senator John O. Pastore and John Fischer help probe the question of bias in television newscasting. (PBL/NET)

Why Are Atoms Unpredictable?   30 min. B & W. Purchase $100; rental $6.25.

Demonstrates the strange and contradictory particle and wave behavior of electrons.

Will the Gator Glades Survive?   30 min. Color. Purchase $315; rental $11.50.

A view of the wildlife inhabiting the Florida Everglades which is in danger because man is interferring with the natural water supply. (NET)

World of Piri Thomas   60 min. Color. Purchase $420; rental $18. B & W. Purchase $240; rental $13.

Piri Thomas is the author of the book *Down These Mean Streets*, and in this film, Thomas takes the viewer on a tour of Spanish Harlem, where two-thirds of the 900,000 Puerto Ricans in the United States live. (NET)

World of the American Craftsman: The World and Work of Barbara Scarponi   28 min. Color. Purchase $315; rental $11.50.

An examination of the art of Barbara Scarponi. Scarponi, who works in wax and metal, is shown casting a ring.

World of the American Craftsman: The World and Work of Dorothy Young   30 min. Color. Purchase $315; rental $11.50.

Dorothy Young is a weaver and throughout this film she discusses the role weaving has played in her life. (ETS/PS)

World of the American Craftsman: The World and Work of Vivika Heino   30 min. Color. Purchase $240; rental $10.

A look at the artists Vivika and Otto Heino, and their pottery making. (ETS/PS)

World of the American Craftsman: The World and Work of Walker Weed 28 min. Color. Purchase $315; rental $11.50.

A look at the art of Walker Weed, and his woodworking accomplishments from skis to furniture.

World of the American Craftsman: The World and Work of Winslow Eaves 29 min. Color. Purchase $240; rental $10.

Winslow Eaves is a sculptor who works in wood, bronze, and steel. At his New Hampshire home he is shown doing bronze casting—exciting, but emotionally exhausting and physically dangerous work.

World of the Weed 21 min. B & W. Purchase $125; rental $5.50.

A history of the original use of the "weed" in the Orient, its travels to other parts of the world, the derivatives of marijuana that have come into use, and the legal and moral problems associated with its use.

Writers: John Updike 30 min. B & W. Purchase $125; rental $6.75.

A series of filmed interviews with John Updike during which the writer discusses some of the beliefs, concepts, and attitudes which have influenced his novels. (NET)

Writers: Philip Roth 30 min. B & W. Purchase $125; rental $6.75.

A conversation between writer Philip Roth and Jerre Mangione, novelist and professor of English at the University of Pennsylvania, during which Roth discusses his stories and plays and explains the covert and ostensible meanings of his works. (NET)

Writers: Science Fiction 30 min. B & W. Purchase $125; rental $6.75.

A discussion of science fiction by a panel of writers, a scientist, and an English professor which includes both historical and future perspective and definitions of science fiction. (NET)

ROCK:
POPULAR MUSIC
IN THE SIXTIES
John Burks

Looking back over these past ten years, it seems ridiculous to lay down an historical overview, because after all, we are dealing here with the songs and sounds that set America in vibration—the mass popular music that is by now our common shared experience. If you missed it, too bad; I can't make it come alive again on the printed page. If it's strictly an historical overview you're after, let me direct you to pages 80 to 93. But there's nothing staler than last week's hit single or last week's hit album or last year's hit performer. And books about them, while they can serve to frame the pop onslaught in some sort of perspective, are, at base, catalogs of dead thrills. Let's sidestep just a moment to look at just one book by way of example. I refer to the *Rock Encyclopedia* by Lillian Roxon, a sweet Australian lady who covers America for one of the newspapers back home and makes it her duty to stay abreast of the doings of all the major rock-and-roll performers.

There are two broad designations of people who write about rock-and-roll. One consists of historians who attempt

John Burks, formerly with *Newsweek* and *Rolling Stone*, is a reporter for the *San Francisco Examiner*.

to deal with rock culture the way a C. Wright Mills or a Theodore White might have done it had he been young and stoned during the 1960s. They are the critics who attempt to write about this stuff on a firm sociological and musicological footing. The other consists of people who write about the pop stars as stars, rather the same way movie magazines write about movie stars, and who write about the music in terms of the ups and downs it brings them personally. The polite way of describing these people is "fans."

Now, who's to say which approach beats the other? Not me. Academicians will naturally favor writers who keep a distance from their material, but that's not the way pop music works. If it gets to you, makes you tingle and dance and hum that song, then you're a fan and why pretend otherwise? The thing to look out for in the writing of hard-core fans is that their adoration of their own personal fave raves for extramusical as well as music reasons often blinds them to the merits of others. Since Miss Roxon is more a fan than either a historian or musicologist, one is advised not to take her judgments as the final nor even the fair word where certain performers are concerned. More importantly, her book was published in 1969, and in the world of pop music that's about eighteen light-years ago. This is not a field where encyclopedias (which are, after all, something like state of the union messages) can be expected to remain fresh during the time it takes to print them and get them out to the bookstores. The only encyclopedia entries that can be expected to stand would be those on Jimi Hendrix and Janis Joplin and Jim Morrison and Otis Redding, because they are dead and the book is closed on them.

As good a definition as I've heard of *pop* comes from Greil Marcus, who is my own favorite writer on the subject of rock and the culture that surrounds it. Marcus writes in *Creem* (vol.3, no.3), which is easily the most vital rock periodical, even surpassing *Rolling Stone*:

> POP is a sense that someone else is missing something, but you're not, and when it really works, it's a sense that someone else is missing something but *we're* not. That

is the spirit that lifted the fifties rockers to fame, that made the Beatles matter, and, like it or not, that makes Grand Funk a bigger draw than any other group in the country.

Accept that and you understand why the big thrills in rock are the ones that lie just around the corner. Drinkers and dopers will understand the folly of wasting too much energy meditating upon yesterday's high. The one that counts is this one right here and now. Ah, but this is sheer hedonism, you say? You're right. They don't sell all those records because it's Art and it's Good for you.

Another way of saying it is the cliché that a performer is only as good as his next record. Who cares that Bill Haley and the Comets sold 46 zillion records back in 1950-something? We already heard that stuff. It's over with. Take us someplace new. That is the real meaning of the term "Rock-and-roll will stand." It's the title of a very early 1960s hit on the Minit label by a New Orleans band called the Showmen. Except for "Rock and Roll Will Stand," you can forget you ever heard of the Showmen for the same reason you can forget Bill Haley. They're yesterday's news. But *Rock and Roll Will Stand,* which is also the title of the best book, for my money, on the subject (assembled by Greil Marcus), is a most paradoxical way of saying what it means: Keep on boppin'—the hits just keep coming. Therein lies the eternal strength of this music—its constancy as a source of new cheap thrills.

The two best ways to grasp what rock-and-roll had become by the end of the 1960s are to see a movie and listen to an album of records. The movie is *Gimme Shelter,* but you shouldn't see it until you've listened to an album of records, *Woodstock,* subtitled *Music from the Original Soundtrack and More* (Cotillion SD 3-500), which comes from the movie of the same name but beats the pants off the movie. The movie seemed endless to me, and preposterously chauvinistic, with its constant gee-whiz-look-at-us.

The record doesn't have Dylan on it because he wasn't at Woodstock, nor does it have the Beatles, who had broken up as a group by that time (1969), nor the Rolling Stones, nor numerous others. What it does have, above and beyond good performances by John Sebastian, Joe Cocker, the Jefferson Airplane, Crosby, Stills, Nash & Young, and Jimi Hendrix's absolutely best recorded performance, is the soaring spirit of rock-and-roll—the promise of sharing, the sense that we're all in this together, the meeting of the musicians and their public—nearly a half million of them—on a once-only totally free basis. The stage announcements, the sound of the crowd, and the vibrance of it make it an almost perfect document of the end of an era—not the end of rock-and-roll, but an end to an *era* of rock-and-roll.

The movie *Gimme Shelter* is the capstone to that era. It should have been called *Altamont,* for that is the event upon which it centers—the massive free one-day rock show conceived and presented by the Rolling Stones to end their 1969 tour of the States. It was held at Altamont, California, in a dusty cowpatch cum stockcar-racing track. What happened there, as surely everybody under the age of fifty must by now know, is that the Hell's Angels, who were supposed to be policing the 300,000 or so who came, instead came on like Attila's legion, terrorizing thousands and beating scores of stoned freaks with pool cues. Finally, they succeeded in stealing the show from the Stones themselves, who were at that very moment performing onstage not 40 feet away, by knifing a young black man to death.

Tons of peace and love and good vibes and flower power and goodness had been attached to the rock-and-roll skyrocket of the 1960s. "Love Is All You Need," sang the Beatles. This was partly out of the high hopes and fantasies of rock's young audience and partly because the record companies saw money to be made by fusing their product with the youth revolution or whatever it was and poured bundles of dollars into promoting the idea that lighting up a joint, with rock-and-roll on the record player, was a shortcut to everything bee-yoo-ti-ful. In one hilarious advertisement Columbia Records depicted a group of longhairs listening to records—the sort of people you see at demonstrations, or playing as members of rock bands, or dealing dope. "The

Man can't bust our music," was the headline. That whole myth came tumbling down at Altamont. The movie shows you the exact moment, as knife blades glint and a man falls dying.

The movie *Gimme Shelter* is a good metaphor for the 1960s generally. Despite all our cultural and scientific achievements during the decade, Death kept sticking his head in the door and saying, "Hey, look, you creeps are just animals after all." The Kennedy assassinations, the Malcolm X assassination, the Martin Luther King assassination, the murders of scores of black (and white) people in the South, and, most importantly, the war in Vietnam mocked all our American triumphs at decade's end and left the nation not only divided but also unsure of its direction and increasingly disbelieving of its leaders.

Altamont was rock-and-roll's Vietnam, in the sense that Altamont cast the gravest doubts on all that had preceded it. So this is what it comes to? Was it worth it? How could we allow it? These unanswerables plagued the fans and the businessmen of rock mightily. The Rolling Stones came out of it all with an image so bad it made the Beatles look like choirboys. If you don't trust the Stones, who can you trust? After Altamont, nobody.

Just a few months into the new decade (the date was May 31, 1971, as a matter of fact) Columbia Records president Clive J. Davis sent out a press release in which he attempted to put an end to the recurrent rock-is-dying theme. "Those," he wrote, "who are sounding a premature death knell really must not be permitted to put the vigor, the ingenuity, the creativeness of today's music in a negative posture." "Its life force," he continued, "is flowing as strong as ever but it's touching on new and ever-changing boundaries." Everything changes, Davis went on, nothing remains the same forever, and "what is happening now is the emergence of the song, of the beautiful material that is the essence of music." People like James Taylor, Carole King, Laura Nyro, and Elton John "are speaking out," said Davis, "and they undoubtedly will join Bob Dylan, Paul Simon, and McCartney and Lennon as the poet laureates of our times." Song and poetry are, of course, two entirely different matters. Davis' statement illustrates the mushiness at the top of the record biz. It is also worth noting that the two most dubious entries on Davis' list of "laureates" present and future—Nyro and Simon—record for his label. But then so does Dylan.

The point is that it does very little good to talk with industry figures or even musicians about the future of rock and ·pop. They don't know. They do know that they hope their music is headed for Number One. But if they really knew where the bandwagon was headed, they wouldn't be standing around talking about it, they'd already have recorded it. A quantum jump, like the Beatles' *Sgt. Pepper's Lonely Hearts Club Band* (Capitol 2653) or Dylan's *Blonde on Blonde* (Columbia C2S 841) comes as a big surprise. It wasn't what you expected. If you'd been expecting it, you wouldn't have gotten such a cheap thrill off it. Chances are that the guy who can tell us what the next Big Thrill will be, because he's the guy who's going to create it, is somebody we never heard of.

Back to Clive Davis, head of Columbia Records: "No, contemporary rock music is not dying. It is just weeding out the lesser lights by a process of elimination and the entrance fee is growing higher. But it is here to stay . . . . Creative genius is flourishing. Keen consumer interest is abundant. And there sure is a lot more to say."

In the same mail came *Circular,* the weekly public relations leaflet from Warner Bros. Records, which had surer and cuter prose. Dated June 7, 1971, and headlined "WB Refuses to Put Out," the explanatory blurb went like this:

> In a precedented move, Warner Bros. Records has refused flatly to issue a June, 1971, album release. Albums heretofore scheduled for that spring month have been deferred to future monthly releases. Commenting on this refusal, one highly placed company source stated, "Sure thing we're skipping June. We're skipping it till America wakes up to its senses and starts buying up all the good stuff we've put out for the first half of '71." Industry figures, who refused to be quoted, noted that WBR executives indeed seemed miffed that eleven of its albums, each of which had received critical acclaim and heavy

airplay, had not yet sold enough to become gold album award recipients and hang in the upstairs hallway because of it . . . . Pushy force behind the June ban of new albums from Burbank is the record company's curly-haired sales head, E. Rosenblatt. Reliable reports state that when Rosenblatt saw the heavy June schedule of new talent set for new albums, the sales mogul exclaimed, "Ye Gods. We're still working on albums from last January, fellas!" and then, they say, he crossed his eyes.

By now, all eleven of those albums have been released, though none of them have exactly set the world afire, let alone "sold enough to become gold album award recipients and hang in the upstairs hallway because of it." With the exception of the *Crazy Horse* and *Small Faces* albums, it was a most unextraordinary release of music for a company like Warner's that has built its excellent reputation on well-produced and satisfying performances from artists carefully nurtured to stardom by WB's media experts. It was a typical lineup, neither better nor worse than the industry has been coming up with of late.

The problem is that so much of the music sounds just like something you already heard. As long as that's the case, it's unlikely that America will come to its senses and start buying—at least, not like America was buying during the 1960s. A study done by the CBS/Columbia Group Market research department on the occasion of Columbia Records' eightieth anniversary, however, showed that the record industry "pushed ahead" to new high sales levels every year of the past decade. In 1967, before recorded tapes were a factor in sales, the industry passed the billion-dollar sales mark for recorded discs. By 1969 the industry's total sales of recorded tapes and records combined exceeded $1.5 billion. The record industry's growth rate far exceed most measures of the nation's economic growth. Sales were up from $610 million in 1960 to $1.58 billion in 1969—a jump of 160 percent. The gross national product increased half as fast.

Nobody keeps a full count of the number of companies manufacturing records and tapes and the companies that service those companies, but the trade publication *Cash Box* came up with these estimates: 1,363 record manufacturers, 981 distribution agencies, 249 recording studios, 144 record presses, 40 record plating plants and machine shops, 52 record sleeve manufacturers, 22 album jacket printers and lithographers. In 1960 half of the nation's households owned a record player. Now over 75 percent of all homes have them— and a significant percentage owns two or more. "The best guess," Columbia's market research group concludes, "as to the trend of the industry in the 1970s predicts that record sales will continue to advance at a rate about the same as that experienced in the 1960s." This would mean that the $1.8 billion sales for 1970 indicates something like $5.4 billion for 1980.

One of the things this article pretends to do is to predict where rock-and-roll, which is directly responsible for the recording industry's growth, is headed. So it's time to explore trends. Without pretending in any way that what follows is a "Concise History of Rock and Roll," let me sketch a few of the major developments of the 1960s and try to guess what they might hold for the future.

Although Janis Joplin, Jimi Hendrix, and Jim Morrison each had a considerable impact on the rock of the later 1960s, the three of them are dead. Janis and Jimi died within a month of one another, as 1970 was sputtering toward its end, and Morrison in mid-1971. None of them were yet thirty, a fact which inspired a fair amount of sloppy warrior-who-died-young prose. As to what killed them: Hendrix' management managed to convince everybody that the prince of electric voodoo guitar choked on some sleeping pills. Joplin's management reportedly managed to clean up her room so only a discreet amount of heroin was found. The autopsy said an overdose did her in. This surprised almost everybody, except only the super hip, who claim to know that she was on smack because if they didn't know that they wouldn't qualify for super-hip status. Janis, of course, was a boozer. At least that was her stage persona—belting out those whoa-poor-me grinders and guzzling a bottle of Southern Comfort. Jim Morrison, too, had acquired no little reputation as a lush. When he died they buried him quietly and then told the press about it, with nothing more than "natural causes" for an explanation.

Now, then, who were these people, and what did they mean to the music? Starting with the least important, in terms of his continuing influence, we turn to Jim Morrison, headman and lead singer of the Doors, a Los Angeles band that specialized in rock as theater. Actually it was Morrison who did that. The band just pumped away in the background in phlegmatic, though loud, repetition. Morrison was the Doors' whole act, and his act consisted of pacing the stage with a hand mike, spinning out badinage ("Wanna see my cock?") from behind his snakeskin and leather clothes. There was a big furor in Miami when he was said to have exhibited his reproductive apparatus to an overflow audience, precipitating a reaction from decent, crew-cut youngsters in the form of decency rallies held at major football stadiums. One of the biggest backers of these rallies was the comedian Jackie Gleason, himself a big-time drinker like Morrison. But booze was not enough to bridge the gap between them.

Morrison's posture was that of Rock Superstar. While he was neither the best at the act (Mick Jagger is probably Number One, though this ranking should not be mistaken for any sort of praise) nor the first (Elvis came first), Morrison was assuredly the creepiest, inspiring imitation from a legion of creeps. The creepiest surviving practitioner of this art is Iggy of Iggy and the Stooges, formerly the Psychedelic Stooges of Detroit, who is not only a miserable singer, but whose band is even worse. Iggy's whole act consists of howling and shrieking into a microphone while he prances the stage shirtless in skin tight leather trousers and pantomimes absurd sexual confrontations with the mike. At least the Doors had a few songs, most notably "Light My Fire," to be heard on their first album, *The Doors* (Elektra EKL 4007). The Stooges ain't got nothing except Iggy's dynamic posturings, and that's good news, because it means that rock as theater has been reduced to its absolute and final bones and doesn't figure as a trend of any importance for the 1970s. Except, of course, for Mick Jagger and the Rolling Stones, but that's a different story. Jagger will probably always do what he's always done—bad-boy unisex prance and stomp, singing it as black and nasty as a white British rocker can, but that's just him, it's not rockers by the dozens.

Much has been said about Janis Joplin's likeness to Billie Holiday. She had no likeness to Billie Holliday in any way whatsoever at all, except they both drank too much and had scratchy voices. The essence of Billie's artistry was her absolute control and mastery of her material, bending it, reshaping it, making gems of trifling songs (like "Miss Jones to You"), and turning good songs ("Strange Fruit," "All of Me," dozens of others) into personal triumphs of such perfection that other singers were scared to touch them.

Janis did a whole other thing. Just the titles of the songs she was best known for ("Pieces of My Heart," "Ball and Chain," "I Need a Man to Love") suggest what she was up to, and Janis can best be heard on the *Big Brother and the Holding Company* album (Columbia KCS 9700). She'd take any song that had the makings and turn it into an ear-splitting hymn of pain and sexual yearning—pressing her own emotions to the edge. Punctuating the whole thing with screams and cries and moans, Janis sounded like she was out of control, in the grip of passions too fierce to bear. It was this quality, more than the (satiric?) sexuality of her whore-styled costumes and her wildly disarrayed hair, that made her audience, in her words, "want to ball me."

What I am saying is that Janis was only partly a musical success, though she could do stunning things with her voice. More importantly, she was a show business success. When she died, her act died with her and her impact on other singers has been nil. But her sartorial impact on the generation of fans remains, at this writing, almost as strong as it was a couple of years ago. It may be that Janis defined better than anybody else the freak look of the latter 1960s for women. She's as immortal as the Flapper Girl, and the fashion magazines ran dozens of photos of her. She had style.

Hendrix was the male equivalent of Janis when it came to clothes and hair. His corona of Afro-styled hair was unparalleled when Jimi turned up in 1967, fresh from England (where he'd gone to make a name for himself, to return home triumphant as Robert Frost had done decades earlier) in his psychedelic Jean LaFitte-styled post-mod attire. The difference is that Hendrix was an original, musically speaking. Janis took a lot of things other (black) people had done before her and put her own frenzy to them. Jimi Hendrix created a whole new electronic language for guitar. There were plenty of others who played with wah-wah pedals (which create something like that sound of wah-wah on trombone or trumpet), feedback, and lots of amplifiers and speakers, but none was so uniquely gifted at turning this noisemaking apparatus toward real musical ends.

Rock-and-roll owes everything to black music, and Hendrix, himself black, owed his music to this tradition as well. What makes him unusual among the 1960s rockers is that he extended the music, where most rock-and-rollers only borrowed. (It's also interesting to contrast Joe Cocker, who reached a considerable peak of super-stardom at the end of the decade, at the same time as Jimi Hendrix. Cocker had the gorgeous arrangements of Leon Russell to set off his stylings, which went basically the way Ray Charles, the great pioneer soul singer, would have sung them if he'd felt like it. Cocker, like his audience, is young, longhaired, and white. An 18-year-old girl can identify with him. She can't identify with Ray Charles, who's 40-something, blind, black, and wears a business suit and tie when he performs. She can dig Ray Charles, but she can get excited over Joe Cocker. To sample this peculiar phenomenon, hear Cocker's *With a Little Help from My Friends,* A&M Records SP 4182.)

While he lived, Jimi Hendrix was rock-and-roll's heaviest male sex symbol. It might be argued that Mick Jagger was heavier, but his appeal is really unisexual. This appeal really was Jimi's image, his act. Like Joplin's act, it died when he died. In rock-and-roll there is surprisingly little of the kind of graveyard adulation that followed the deaths of earlier youth superstars like James Dean. Hendrix does not loom larger than life to his legions of fans. In fact, I'd say he looms considerably smaller. The whole Hendrix mythology had blown him out of all human proportion, and with his death his fans saw that Jimi was mortal after all. And . . . life goes on . . .

where's the next kick coming from? This is *not* to say that the rock-and-roll community is so callous that no sorrow was felt when Hendrix (and Joplin) died. But it didn't last long. Hendrix's posthumous album, like Joplin's, was a gold record before it was even released—wholesalers had already sold a million's worth to the record stores before the official release date—but, given his popularity, that would have happened anyway, just because it was a new Hendrix album. There is, after all, an increasing suspicion about heroes and a lack of inclination to help create them, and maybe it's just as well. Digging a performer's star trip is quite a different thing from worshipping a hero. A hero has to be real. A star only has to be a star.

The most important thing about Hendrix is his music. In case you think that Hendrix just sort of emerged, came from out of nowhere, listening closely to John Lee Hooker's earlier work will tell you a lot about Hendrix's roots. You ought also to listen to John Coltrane's band with Elvin Jones on drums to hear a precedent, perhaps an inspiration, for the interplay and dynamism between Hendrix and Mitch Mitchell, drummer in Jimi's band, the Experience.

Hooker represents some of the roughest and most antique blues still being performed; it has been said that some of his model-like drone blues work matches exactly guitar and vocal music played by southern blacks during the 1870s and 1880s. Coltrane was, of course, the major jazz figure of the 1960s, the man who invented a whole new language for tenor saxophone in something like the same way Hendrix found new voices in the guitar. Between Hooker and Coltrane the extremes of black American music are covered, and that is precisely what Jimi Hendrix did. But he was no eclectic.

In much the same way that Charlie Parker, the great bebop alto saxophonist of the 1940s, took the funkiest and the most cerebral elements of jazz and recast the whole of it into a brand-new, totally forward-looking music, Hendrix put a new face on rock-and-roll.

His accomplishment was unlike the Beatles'. They combined a talent for song writing with humor and a knack for packaging diverse sounds and music into mind-blowing servings. The Beatles were important for the way they derailed all concepts of what rock-and-roll ought to be. The result could be a song about a street they'd grown up on, or it could be about a walrus and told in lyric poetry that came closer to Corso than to Ira Gershwin.

Since my purpose in this article is to talk about the old rock-and-roll of the 1960s in terms of its impact on the new music of the 1970s, there's not a lot more to say about the Beatles here. Suffice it to say that their acclaim, and later, their inventiveness, constantly busting apart old song forms to reassemble them in wholly unexpected and wholly right shapes, set the standard for the music and the superstar trip that followed in the wake of their unparalleled impact. But the superstar routine, despite everything the record companies have done and continue to do to hype it, seems to be waning. There's only room for one Marilyn Monroe every six or seven years is the way the cliché goes. Yet the latter 1960s produced such a glut of rock-and-roll superstars (Jimi, Janis, Mick Jagger, the Beatles, Morrison, ad infinitum) that an overdose seems to have resulted. Will the withdrawal be painful? It's going to be painful for a lot of used-up superstars. One of them—who got a bundle of money for signing with one of the very biggest record companies and whose high-energy performances put him into the big leagues for almost two years—is presently holed up at home, trying to find some way to end his compulsive heroin habit, vowing never to play music again. Corny as this story may sound, it's true and typical.

Fans have been buying somewhat less of the music whose principal claim is that a superstar is making that music. This is a hopeful sign for the 1970s. But let us not forget that superstars can be made good use of. An example of this is Chess Records *The Howlin' Wolf Sessions* (CH 60008). Howlin' Wolf, the roughest and toughest of contemporary blues singers, whose songs, like "Smokestack Lightnin'" and "Sittin' on Top of the World," have been recorded by countless blues-rock white folks, is accompanied by a panorama of superstars: Eric Clapton, superstar lead guitarist of the late and fantastically profitable supergroup Cream; Steve Winwood, superstar keyboard player known as Stevie when he was part of the late, and mellow, supergroup called Traffic; and Bill Syman on bass and Charlie Watts on drums, two superstars by virtue of being Rolling Stones; plus, on one song, Ringo Starr, the superstar drummer of the world's champion superstar Beatles. The idea here was to match a matchless master of the blues with the rockers who are so much in his debt. I assume this will mean that many times more people will hear Howlin' Wolf than ever in his lifetime because of the superstars who appear with him.

On the album the superstars behave themselves, working to give Wolf the toughest support they know how, and they know how to pretty well, because they cut their teeth on the music of Howlin' Wolf and Muddy Waters and Jimmy Reed and B.B. and Albert King and Bo Diddley and Chuck Berry and Little Richard and Little Walter and all the other great originals. So we are afforded a good chance to hear Howlin' Wolf in a sympathetic setting. At the same time, this record offers convincing proof that the blues-rockers have carried their scene as far as it will go, for old Howlin' Wolf, nearly sixty, walks away with it. He shines so brightly that these kids sound half dead. Virtuosos though they are, they don't sound half as good to me as the musicians Howlin' Wolf usually records with—obscure Chicagoans whose names are unknown outside a small circle of blues freaks. Compare for yourself. Listen to Wolf's album called *Evil* (Chess 1540), recorded between 1951 and 1959. The accompaniment is crude. They sometimes miss the notes but they never quit stomping. Then listen to the newer album, where these British boys never miss a note. They play it perfect and sometimes they even play it tough, but it's a telling contrast. If you're interested in the *Howlin' Wolf Sessions* LP, don't let my criticism scare you off. Wolf's backing is a mite pallid, but his presence makes it worthwhile.

I am of two minds. On one hand, I think it's awfully nice that the Rolling Stones have recorded so much blues, that they were reasonably true to the music and didn't go for a lot of gimmicks, and that they turned a lot of people on to the real thing. But only the very best of the Stones even begins to compare with the originality and vitality of the real bluesmen. The Stones are at their strongest, to my mind, on *Beggar's Banquet* (London PL 53), and especially the track "Sympathy for the Devil," where the band chugs along something like Muddy Waters' band in full flight—perhaps a bit lighter—with lyrics that are winningly and lastingly sardonic.

It's a typical Stones performance, in that Mick Jagger's vocal is buried back so far in the mix of instruments that it's very difficult to be sure what the words are. This is a little device the Stones cunningly cooked up to gauze over lyrics that might be a little tricky for radio airplay (like "Let's Spend the Night Together"). At least that's one explanation for it. Another is that Jagger's menacing, but thin, voice is more effective by implication than head on. Dig the difference, if you will, between the recorded Jagger and the recorded Howlin' Wolf or Muddy Waters. The voices of the bluesmen are recorded way out front of the band and all but explode from the speakers.

Musically, the Stones would appear to have reached the end of the line. Their last couple of albums sound like a lot of stuff you have already heard before. Still, they have acquired the mantle of "The World's Greatest Rock and Roll Band—I forget who first called them that—and present themselves as a band to be watched. Every album comes at you saying in pop's best tradition: Dig this. This is where it's at. Take a look at their latest album's cover—the *Sticky Fingers* album (Rolling Stones Records COC 5910)—depicting the front of a young man's jeans, with a real zipper, which can be unzipped to reveal underwear pants. Andy Worhol designed it. As graphics, it's terrific. As morality or whatever you want to call it, the Stones likely want us to think this is where it's at, or will be at. Pure and funky street eros, or something. So the Stones remain, as always, superb strategists. Never mind that they may be almost total strangers to the fans of Grand Funk Railroad.

Rock-and-roll of the 1970s, I believe, will be more of the same, that is, it will be more electronically amplified music made by young white people for young white people borrowing heavily from country and mountain music of an earlier America and borrowing especially heavily from black American music: from blues, jazz, and soul music. The middle-class nature of American youth assures that they will never respond in large numbers to "low class" country and western music. And our continuing racism assures that they'll embrace dozens more Bob Dylans and Mick Jaggers before they even get to know the names of John Coltrane and Clifton Chenier or Little Walter—or the 1975 equivalents of those gifted black men. The real aesthetic tragedy of Jimi Hendrix's death is that the power of his music was such that it could have made black music of all sorts accessible to rock-and-roll's young white audience. There's a gap there that Hendrix might have helped to bridge, and thereby to have brought popular appeal and economic benefits to the men who invented this music.

A Review

PEOPLE AND SCENES

San Francisco. Because there was so much activity in this city, the media came up with a label, "The San Francisco Sound." It never had any substance—there never was any identifiable San Francisco sound. There were a lot of rock-and-roll bands that sounded nothing at all like one another. The endless electric mandala-like unwebbing of the Grateful Dead bore no resemblance to the rockified outerspace electric folk music trip of the Jefferson Airplane, except perhaps that both fell under the even more general term: "acid rock." This was because the musicians and their audience took a lot of LSD, not because of any common fabric in the music. Big Brother's apocalyptic shrill had nothing to do with Quick-silver Messenger Service's static Bo Diddley derivations. Creedence Clearwater and the Steve Miller Band were about as far apart as the Bayou is from Chicago, though they did have the blues in one form or another in common. And I could go on, but why? San Francisco was most important as an audience and for the Fillmore West rock-and-roll ballroom operation of Bill Graham, who made few friends while he made his million proving he sure knew how to put on a show. Graham, whose Fillmores became as well known as Woodstock and were probably more influential, decided in 1971 that the audience had turned into a bunch of creeps—mainly because of the community's heavy drug use and failure to concern itself with any of the major social issues—and shut down his halls.

Soul Music. By "soul music" is meant the latter-day extension of what used to be called rhythm and blues. In general terms, it's the stuff they play on black radio stations. It owes something to black gospel music, something to the blues and something to jazz. In its latest emanation, soul music reached its high at about the time of Aretha Franklin's "Chain of Fools" and Otis Redding's "Dock of the Bay," the 1967–68 period. It was too high to get any higher. There was no way to get more gospel in there, no way to make it funkier (you've got to hear Otis' *Live in Europe* album, Velt Records S-416) than that. Well, maybe Otis would have gotten beyond that plateau, but he died in 1968, of success. He'd just had his first big national acclaim and was rolling in enough dough that he felt like showing it off. He bought himself a jet plane to get from job to job and on the very first tour with it, bam, into a lake, Otis Redding dead at age twenty-six; the same age as Jimi Hendrix, and the same potential importance musically, too. This is not to say there are no interesting soul performers remaining. Aretha has cooled down, but Roberta Flack is great—she's everything Nina Simone ought to be. She's young, she writes fine material, and she blends drama and musicianship beautifully. But is she going to have the kind of impact on soul music that Otis and Aretha had? Roberta doesn't seem either individual or overpowering enough.

Sly and the Family Stone. That's the full name of his band. The album to hear is called *Stand!* (Epic Records BN-26456). Though Sly's audience was largest among the rock-and-roll set, *Stand!* stood the reigning geniuses of soul music business on their ear, especially the producers and executives at Atlantic and at Motown Records. Sly's impact on soul music has been much like the Beatles' on rock—expanding, reordering and reshaping the music to give it more possibilities than had ever occurred to anybody before. His lyrics are repetitive and pat:

> Pretty, pretty, pretty as a picture
> Witty, witty, witty as you can be
> Blind, 'cause your eyes see only glitter
> Closed to the things that make you free

But, as with the best pop music, it's the sound of it that counts, and Sly gets his sound by means of a dense overlay of incongruities. He'll backdrop an electronic microphone solo—it's Sly, scatting into a microphone, equipped with a wah-wah pedal to distort and distend its sound—with group chanting, military drums, a bass line straight out of Muddy Waters' "Rollin' and Tumblin'," and a trumpet playing wispy atonal side melodies. This is all edited and spliced together in such a way that you simply cannot imagine what to expect next, until you get to "know" the song. On the heels of *Stand!* everybody was tossing some Sly licks into his act. But its been two years now since Sly released that *Stand!* He's a slow worker in the recording studio and a quirky personality to boot. It's not a question whether Sly can be influential—he will be perhaps crucially so if his output is sufficient to keep him ahead of the traffic.

Dylan. At this stage in the life of Bob Dylan it's hard to see that he's got anything important remaining to tell us. His last three or four albums have been abysmal. They have sent the critics into varying flights of ecstasy, panic, confusion, and forty-seven other varieties. But the simple fact is that since *John Wesley Harding* (Columbia Records CS 9604), Dylan's lost the enigmatic oracular quality that made him seem to speak for his whole generation:

> Ah, get born, keep warm
> Short pants, learn to dance
> Get dressed, get blessed
> Try to be a success
> Please her, please him, buy gifts
> Don't steal, don't lift

Twenty years of schoolin'
and they put you on the day shift
Look out kid, they keep it all hid
Better jump down a manhole
Light yourself a candle, don't wear sandals
Try to avoid the scandals
Don't wanna be a bum
You better chew gum
The pump won't work
'Cause the vandals took the handles

That was 1965 and the song was "Subterranean Homesick Blues," and it was just one of dozens that Dylan gave us to provide young people with whole new turns of phrase and ways of seeing. Not only that, but his songs cooked—they bopped right along, and you could, if you wanted, dance and even hum along. Quite different from 1970, when we found Dylan recording "Blue Moon." It would be nice to have a figure similar to the visionary mid-1960s Dylan on the scene right now, to make some sense out of it. But Dylan ain't interested. If you want to feel what it felt like when Dylan had us in the palm of his hand, you have got to get hold of *Bringing It All Back Home Again* (Columbia CS 9128) and *Blonde on Blonde* (Columbia C2S 841). Then if you want to explore into the past to see where Dylan's roots lie, dig Woody Guthrie's *Dust Bowl Ballads* (RCA Records Vintage Series LPV-502), filled with topical songs from America's Depression balladeer, Dylan's spiritual father. And if you want to go farther back yet, listen to Early Rural String Bands (also on RCA Vintage Series LPV-552), which dates back to 1922–49 and provides the whole under-pinning for folk-rock, which is sort of Dylan's thing. Dylan has recorded with lots of country musicians. But that's not why I include this record on my list. It's there because the roots of this music give as good an indication of what tomorrow holds as anything contemporary. *Ballads and Breakdowns of the Golden Era*, a Columbia Records compilation from 1927–31 period, is worth your while for the same reason.

The Band. These are five guys who used to be Dylan's back-up band and a mighty band they are. Few albums are filled with more gothic promise than theirs. Forget the album numbers, buy all three albums. They're on Capitol. Their sound is as countrified as rock-and-roll gets, their rhythm section is super-charged (not unlike the better soul bands), and they have the highest, most bittersweet blending and tangling of voices in modern music. Their songs are chock-full of American mystery-dream-promise images and it's hard to find a single thing wrong with The Band except that they, like Sly Stone, seem to be in doldrums. It's been too many months since they confronted us with new riddles to dance and sing. You have the feeling that they, like Sly, could be tremendously important to the direction the music will take, if they choose to. But will they?

Jazz-Rock. It never even got off the ground. Yes, there is a band called Blood Sweat & Tears that has had four outrageously successful albums on the market. But when you listen to the "jazz" solos by BS&T's young white players and then listen to some real jazzmen doing their stuff . . . well, weak as BS&T (and Chicago and numerous other "jazz-rock" bands) play it, it just doesn't seem fair to call it jazz. If it's called jazz-rock, you can pretty safely ignore it. But it will reward you to hear what's going on in Jazz now, because what's happening in jazz today will likely be reflected in rock sooner or later. Indeed, I would go farther than that: here's some jazz that you ought to hear because it's great, and then later, when the rockers get around to stealing licks, you can say, "I already heard that stuff."

JAZZ

Miles Davis at Fillmore (Columbia G-30038) shows his band all trapped out in electronic devices, with two percussionists, playing long, free-form improvisations totally exotic in setting and direction. Miles is Miles, ever changing, and this is one of his most exciting changes. You ask yourself, how could Miles get farther out than this? The answer is almost certainly forthcoming.

The Jazz Composer's Orchestra (JCOA Records 1001/2) features that large cooperative ensemble with terrifically emotional playing by avant-garde jazz's most expressive musicians —Don Cherry, Roswell Rudd, Pharoah Sanders, Larry Coryell, Gato Barbieri, and especially Cecil Taylor.

A Love Supreme by John Coltrane (Impulse Records Stereo A-77) is in many ways the essential Coltrane album, a religious statement vibrant with the emotional force of Coltrane's horn and his band's polyrhythmics. Coltrane's extended excursions, his multinoted flights, have already been echoed in rock-and-roll guitar improvisations, though this is rather like saying Stravinsky had an impact on radio commercials. A stronger influence was that of Elvin Jones, Coltrane's drummer, on rock drummers, especially Mitch Mitchell, Jimi Hendrix's percussionist. It would have been something to have heard Hendrix and Coltrane jam together. In musical terms they'd have gotten along just fine. To many jazz fans Hendrix the guitar player was a jazz innovator of the first rank, and he won *Down Beat* magazine's Hall of Fame poll.

Live in Seattle is another Coltrane album that should not be missed (Impulse AS-9202-2), featuring Pharoah Sanders and Coltrane on tenor saxophones and Donald Garrett playing the most unearthly bass clarinet ever heard. This is music of the spheres. It is the logical extension of Coltrane's most avant-garde playing, but so far beyond his other recorded work that it seems almost like a new music. The horns and the rhythm bounce off each other like a speeded-up aural kaleidoscope. If rock-and-roll ever gets this advanced—and has a mass following—we will be living on a new planet.

Karma is Pharoah Sanders' own album (Impulse A-9181), released in 1969, two years after Coltrane's death, and very much in the spirit of *A Love Supreme*. It is a gorgeous record with a masterful vocal by Leon Thomas ("The creator has a master plan/Peace and happiness for every man . . . ") and, with its steady rolling rhythm, is what jazz-rock would sound like if it worked. But Pharoah plays jazz, not rock. His tone is so gritty you can almost strike a match on it and mighty sweet, too.

Free Jazz (Atlantic 1364) is one of Ornette Coleman's most exciting outings, featuring two drummers, two bass players, two reed men (Coleman on alto saxophone and the astonishing Eric Dolphy on bass clarinet) and two trumpet players. Ornette is the pioneering figure in the "new jazz," having started playing "free"—sans chord changes or fixed rhythmic patterns—during the late 1950s. On this record everybody plays simultaneously and collectively most of the time, with the featured soloist standing out a bit in front of the swirling, explosive ensemble. A volcano of a recording.

CLASSICS

If you want to compare Janis Joplin and Billie Holiday, you'll need to hear Billie Holiday. Two of the best are *Billie Holiday's Greatest Hits* (Columbia CL 2666) and *Lady in Satin* (Columbia CL 1157).

If you had to pick just two Jimi Hendrix albums for study, they should be *Electric Ladyland* (Reprise 6307) and *Jimi Hendrix Experience Smash Hits* (Reprise 2025).

Charlie Christian invented the way American music is played on electric guitar—which in itself is enough to place two generations of jazz, blues, and pop musicians in his debt—and he was also a brilliant improviser, a precursor of the revolutionary changes that became bebop. His finest hour on record is on the Everest Archive of Folk & Jazz Music Album *Charlie Christian* (FS 219), recorded not long before his death in 1941.

You might as well plunge into the maelstrom of bebop itself. The Savoy Album called *The Charlie Parker Story* (MG 12079) is immodestly, perhaps, but correctly, subtitled "the world's greatest recording session," and it is totally fascinating. You hear Bird (as Parker was called) working out on many versions of the same song, his invention always at the highest level, not to mention his emotion. If you want to know why people laugh at Blood Sweat & Tears, dig Bird.

SOFT PARANOIA

Big record sales at the start of the 1970s have been the good luck of solo performers who play their guitars and sing their songs to the people. The number one name in this field is James Taylor, a nice guy who's got long hair and a pleasant voice, who's been in and out of mental institutions, and who sings songs about his everyday hangups and his love life and tensions and doubts and fears and makes you feel sorry for him. He did this best on a song called "Fire and Rain" which tells about a girl he met while institutionalized who committed suicide. Well, he's seen fire and he's seen rain, but he never thought he'd never see her again. This poor-sensitive-me routine sung over thrumming guitar is fundamentally a holdover from the old folk music days. It's the same music, really, with paranoid lyrics inserted. The names of some other players are Laura Nyro, Melanie and Carly Simon, and gee they're sad. Also Crosby, Stills, Nash & Young who made a bundle, then disbanded. There will always be a place in pop music for troubadors and weepers. But this set has already made its headlines.

Grand Funk Railroad. "Grand Funk Railroad, who sold 10 million records last year and are now debatedly the biggest group in the world, even though: (1) Their music is not played on FM radio. (2) Their music is not played on AM radio. (3) Their records are panned or ignored by the rock press. (4) Many people who care about rock-and-roll don't listen to them. (5) Some people who care about rock-and-roll have never heard of them." This is Greil Marcus in the June, 1971, *Creem,* writing a lengthy piece called "Rock-A-Hula Clarified" that is the best piece on rock-and-roll I've ever read, attempting as it does to put everything straight. Because it's Greil Marcus in the driver's seat, he just about gets there. Grand Funk is extremely low on any of the qualities that I would be inclined to call "musical." They play really loud and really stupid (I was going to say "simply," but that would be lying), but to Marcus that's not the point. He writes:

> The argument against Grand Funk is essentially an art argument that comes out of a claim that rock-and-roll should be art and a conviction that Art Is Good For You. Rock-and-roll, however, is noise, fun, and sound, before it is anything else. Grand Funk may not be art but they are certainly rock-and-roll. No one has ever proved that un-art is bad for you; as Pauline Kael argues, trash

can give us an appetite for art, which is, in fact, precisely what rock-and-roll *does*.

"It doesn't matter," a fan of Grand Funk has written, "if their music isn't as skillful as others. I think that it's a free experience—that's what revolution is all about. We're after the kind of freedom that you feel when you completely lose yourself at a rock concert. There is totally nothing else in your mind or in your head, you aren't even aware of your *body*." Because their music is so devoid of "music"—by which I mean melodic flow and invention and wit and rhythm—it is hard to see what force Grand Funk will exert on the rock of the 1970s, unless a new Dark Ages is coming. Which is always a possibility.

The Beatles. Though it was some time before anybody knew about it, the Beatles broke up, for all practical purposes, in 1968. They made some records after that but the thrill was gone, then the spirit "Hey Jude" went too, gradually, and then acrimony started. Paul McCartney may or may not be the bad guy in the breakup—indications are that his ego was to blame, but John Lennon's ego ain't exactly puny—but however it happened, it happened, and the lovable moptops in whose image the rock-and-roll renaissance of 1965–68 was formed ceased to exist as a musical entity. Each of them put on a new face and started putting out his own records.

The drummer, Ringo Starr, has done some stuff rather along the lines of Frank Sinatra, which is pure goof and laughable. The uncomfortable question is whether Ringo knows they're funny in the way they're funny: peculiar.

Guitarist George Harrison's been more interesting with his India-influenced spirit music, but his latter stuff doesn't stick to the ribs either.

Bassist-composer Paul McCartney is, for me, the saddest of the bunch, having turned out two albums that attempt to recapture the golden giddy glories of the old sweet Beatles days when they couldn't make a record without making a million. He strains so hard for Top Forty lightheartedness, but the magic isn't there. It's like Debbie Reynolds still insisting on teen-age roles or something. Truly pathetic.

John Lennon, on the other hand, is working really hard at being a Fully Realized Adult. His most recent couple of albums are the stuff of psychoanalysis—indeed, Lennon has said as much. There's a whole lot of searing self-confrontation and cunning role playing set against marvelous melodies and textures, and the whole package is certainly intense. In fact, when you're in the right frame of mind, it can be intensely attractive. It's so deeply personal that it's very difficult to say whether Lennon is dealing with our future or his own. If it's ours, it's pop. If it's just his own, it might be art. Tune in later and find it. Don't ask me.

BOOKS

There are a handful of books that should serve you well, and here they are:

Nobody Waved Good-Bye, a rock-and-roll casualty report, edited by Robert Somma, who is editor of *Fusion* magazine, which is normally too stuffy for my taste. This is a first-rate book on rock's high mortality rate, with thoughtful and even moving interviews and chapters dealing with the deaths of Hendrix, Joplin, Brian Epstein (the manager who was the Beatles' guiding light), and Brian Jones, one of the original Rolling Stones. It's a good deal more than just a death watch, but I'm just going to give you the last sentence in the last chapter: "isn't this death stuff proof positive of the ultimate rip-off of the revolution by rock-and-roll, huh?"

The Sound of the City by Charlie Gillett is one of the wisest books about rock and where it came from, if not one of the best written. On the other hand, *The Rock Story* by Jerry Hopkins is a lot better written, if somewhat less knowing. But I would suggest Greil Marcus' *Rock and Roll Will Stand* plus his *Creem* articles over the Gillett and Hopkins books combined.

Country Music: White Man's Blues by John Grissim is readable and the best survey book on country and western music. If you want to know about rock, you'd better know about country. Too many important figures in rock (Elvis, Jerry Lee Lewis, Carl Perkins, et al.) have come from country beginnings to ignore.

Urban Blues by Charles Kell is the definitive book on the contemporary blues scene—everything you ought to know about the men who were its inventors. They even invented the term "rock and roll." In the old days, it meant sex.

Don't Look Back, a book of stills and a transcript of the soundtrack from the movie of the same name, which starred Bob Dylan, is a quick way of getting yourself into Dylan's trip at the peak of his creative powers and popularity. His interview with a *Time* magazine reporter is worth the price alone. "If I want to find out something I'm not going to read *Time* magazine," Dylan tells the man. "There's no ideas in *Time* magazine, there's just facts."

Richard Goldstein's *The Poetry of Rock* is okay if you want to see the words of seventy-one of rock's anthems. I don't think all of this is poetry by a long shot, but a title like that probably helps sell books.

THE BLUES

The Best of Muddy Waters (Chess LP 1427). Enough said.

The Blues Never Die, Otis Spann (Prestige Records 7391). Spann was Muddy Waters' pianist until he died a couple of years ago, and a great blues pianist. He's heard here in an especially rollicking session with Muddy's band and friends.

Little Walter: Hate to See You Go (Chess 1953). Walter was the absolutely top blues harmonica player of Chicago's vital 1940–50 blues years. This record never lets up and never lets you down.

Wailin' The Blues, Jimmy Reed (Tradition 2069). Actually, any Jimmy Reed album would do just as well. He's solid every time. I picked this one because it's a budget label and because the band's really cooking hard. The strong four-to-the-bar beat Jimmy Reed generates is echoed by rock band after rock band, the Beatles included.

Pop Origins, various artists (Chess LP 1544). Contains songs first recorded by Chess artists (Chuck Berry, Bo Diddley, Howlin' Wolf, Muddy Waters, and others) that were later recorded by rock musicians. To my ears, the old bluesmen cut the kids every time. You be the judge. That's the fun of this album.

Two Robert Johnson LPs—*King of the Delta Blues Singers* (Columbia CL 1654) and *King of the Delta Blues Singers, Vol. II* (Columbia C 30034). These contain the exquisite and ethereal vocals and guitar of our most celebrated—and mysterious—bluesman. Numerous rockers have recorded and imitated his work, yet left untouched the heights and depths Robert Johnson reached. In his blues we hear the full range of possibilities of this music, all that the blues can contain to mean to contemporary music. Robert Johnson had it all. To make his legend perfect, nobody knows just how or where he died, and nobody ever got a photo of him, though he made these records in 1936 and 1937. There *were* cameras then.

Bluebird Blues (RCA Vintage Series LPV-518) is culled from RCA's old 1930–40 Bluebird line and features the likes of Blind Willie McTell, Sleepy John Estes, and Tampa Red, all fine bluesmen recorded in their prime.

RURAL

Cajun Music, The Early '50s (Arhoolie Records 5008). Classic performances of this uniquely rough-edged and melodious Louisiana country dance music which dates all the way back to the French Acadians. Stomps along a lot like rock; and country and western sure owes Cajun plenty, too.

Clifton Chenier's Very Best (Blue Thumb Records BTS 15). Chenier's is a luscious mix of Cajun and blues, served up by a black accordionist and his band. Like the Cajun record above, it's strong stuff and may take some getting used to.

There Must Be More to Love than This by Jerry Lee Lewis (Mercury Records SR 61323). A driving and sentimental collection of country songs by an uninhibited pioneer of rock. There's an awful lot of Jerry Lee Lewis on record, almost all of it just fine.

Best of Buffalo Springfield (ATCO SD-33-283) contains gems from a band that broke up in 1968, but not before it made the most successful fusion of rock and country ever. Some of these guys later joined with others and incorporated into the sweet freak pop amalgam, Crosby, Stills, Nash & Young, a big-money rock phenomenon whose crystalline music was to prove a cul-de-sac. Buffalo Springfield topped

91

them in advance. Listen especially on this album for Steve Stills' song, "For What It's Worth." "Paranoia runs deep/Into your life it will creep," it says, "Something happenin' here/What it is ain't exactly clear." It was a sort of minor anthem for the disaffected of the late sixties.

THE FUTURE

And finally some people upon whose futures the future of rock-and-roll may hang:

After the Gold Rush (Reprise Records 6383) is one of Neil Young's solo albums. Really you should hear all his albums, because they contain some of the best song writing anybody's doing these days. And can he sing. The same could be said for Randy Newman's album, *Randy Newman* (Reprise, 6286), except for his singing.

Sir Douglas Quintet Plus Two—Honkey Blues (Smash Records SRS 67108) contains some perfectly meshed Texas rock, with plenty of high blues shouting and funky, hard rhythm. All of Sir Douglas' albums are solid and all of them wear so well it sometimes makes you think that one day Douglas Sahm will zip up to the top of the charts like he's always wanted to but hasn't, except for the hit single, "She's about a Mover." Maybe he's not sexy looking enough. Dylan thinks he's terrific. Top that.

Leon Russell and the Shelter People (Shelter Records SW 2-8903) shows what a songwriter can do about arranging his songs so they sound brand-new if he's got genius. Russell was the guiding light for Joe Cocker, building some fantastic arrangements to showcase what was an otherwise okay but derivative vocal style.

McGuiness Flint (Capitol SMAS-625) sounds like a bunch of Welsh boys who sing in church every Sunday and then head off to the pub to mow 'em down with hard rockers and blazing ballads. Their problem will be the lack of gimmicks for the public to cling to.

John Cale & Terry Riley, *Church of Anthrax* (Columbia C 30131) has got the most bashing two-piano rock-and-roll jam I ever heard. If I thought there was going to be more like that ahead for the 1970s, I'd say all right! Cale's a rocker,

Riley's mainly known as an avant-garde "serious" musician. A fine meeting.

Trout Mask Replica, Captain Beefheart & His Magic Band (Straight Records STS 1053). For just plain old-fashioned weirdness, you can't beat this one. There's more or less a typical rock-and-roll band instrumentation—guitars, bass, drums, and harmonica—with the Captain himself singing and doubling on saxophone. But there the resemblance stops. In his gravelly basso, Beefheart intones lyrics like:

> Moonlight on Vermont affected everybody
> Even Mrs. Wooten as well as little Nitty
> Even lifebuoy floatin'
> With his little pistol showin'

Well that goes to show you what uh moon can do . . . And so on, until he breaks off into a solo flight on his saxophone, sounding for all the world like Pharoah Sanders' brother, while the madhouse out-of-sync rhythms swirl around his head. Too far out, say a lot of intellectual rock fans. But Beefheart has played this stuff in front of teenage kids, for whom he should be incomprehensible, and they loved it. So who knows, after all?

CINEMA
IN THE
SIXTIES

Charles T. Samuels

Cinema is to the culture of the sixties what rebellion or
ecology is to its life—a prime topic for students, editors, and
opinion-makers. As everyone maintains, film is "the now art."
How much of an art is it? To answer that question, we need
some historical perspective.

Like all arts, film involves entertainment. But since movies
cater to a mass audience with a dazzling assortment of devices, they tempt their makers to define entertainment as the
only goal. Therefore, when art is found in the silent era, save
for a few classics (like *Potemkin, Greed, The Cabinet of
Dr. Caligari*), it consists primarily of fist fights and cavalry
charges, of chases—whether in comedy or melodrama—and
of all the thrills made possible by an editing technique that
frees the human body from its limitations.

But the human mind was generally ignored in this emphasis on action. When mind entered the world of silent film, it
was forced to earn through predictability the same easy acceptance that had naturally been granted all physical excite-

Charles Thomas Samuels writes a regular film column for the
American Scholar and is on the staff of Williams College.

ment. Consequently, few who loved literature, music, and the plastic arts could see cinema as more than a pastime.

Sound seemed to change all this. Now characters could speak their minds, but that proved a mixed blessing. Since they lacked speech, silent-film artists had developed a specifically cinematic vocabulary: of gesture, visual analogy, symbolic lighting, expressive tempo. At the beginning of the sound era, many of these lessons were forgotten. Instead of adding sound to earlier resources, thus enriching film art, profit-hungry producers used sound to turn the medium into a new means of distribution, enlarging the audience by making drama or novels accessible to the similiterate. Moreover, commercial instincts that blocked formal growth also interfered with mature content: early sound films merely added to the visual joy of real-life movement the emotional joy of wish fulfillment. When film first spoke, it told the audience what the audience wanted to hear.

In America, this emphasis on the banal was encouraged by democratic piety. But in Europe, where intellectuals had always shown greater interest in the form, a second, more elite tradition in filmmaking began to develop. Perhaps it was first prominent in France, where men like Jean Renoir or Marcel Carné (aided by his scriptwriter Jacques Prévert) brought to the art a desire not to gratify the audience but to represent something of human existence. Films like Renoir's *Rules of the Game* or Carné's *Children of Paradise* showed that movies could be as fearlessly insightful as novels or plays. Great as these films are, however, they are seldom strikingly cinematic. *Rules of the Game,* for example, has several sequences of outstanding visual impact, especially one in which we discover potential destructiveness in some charming aristocrats when they are seen brutally hunting rabbits. But, for the most part, Renoir's themes and insights in this film are expressed through theatrical dialogue and acting. The same is even truer of Carné.

To establish its own genius, film needed to differentiate itself from theater. So long as it told stories expressed mainly through people speaking to one another, the distinction could never be total—and it must not be forgotten that narrative film is an inescapable mixture of theater (dialogue, action), fiction (description, narration), photography, and certain methods peculiar to itself. But because the form's essence is visual and because sound technology eventually made it possible to shoot films outside the studio, cinema possesses an unparalleled ability to wrest meaning from the seen world. Therefore, cinema began to find itself when it moved away from theater in the direction of documentary.

This development began in Italy after World War II. Masterminded by the scenarist Cesare Zavattini and the director Vittorio De Sica, "Italian neorealism" attempted to redefine the nature of cinematic narrative. Sets, professional actors, and literary dialogue—the paraphernalia of theater employed by men like Renoir and Carné—were replaced by amateurs simulating real-life situations in actual locales. Whereas theatricalism had all too easily aligned cinema with wish-fulfilling romantic best sellers, neorealism recalls the classic function of the novel: bringing the news. Because they had undergone the same experience as the filmmakers, the audiences for neorealism could confirm the accuracy of what they saw. But, as De Sica's career itself shows, the alliance between artist and audience was always bedeviled, and when peace and prosperity returned, Italians who wanted to forget their bitter past demanded ever more comforting and theatrical films. However, neorealism had already made its impact by teaching a generation of directors that film art scrupulously reproduces life, with no more tampering than is needed for narrative coherence.

In America, the neorealist lesson was not quickly applied. Taboos and censorship were too rigid; expenditures were too high to allow experimentation: Hollywood kept selling the old dreams. Therefore, as the critic Robert Warshow argued, art survived in Hollywood mainly in gangster films and westerns, where action ensured enough popularity for directors and writers safely to include in their work some recognition that life isn't pure delight. With the single exception of Orson Welles, the only American directors who matter artistically in the forties and fifties are those, like John Ford or Howard

Hawks, whose involvement in action genres freed them from both censorship and excessive reliance on dialogue.

In Sweden, however, a new artist appeared. Equally familiar with theater and films, Ingmar Bergman began to make movies that combine visual and rhetorical richness with individuality in point of view. Bergman's films marked the establishment of the director as an independent creator. Since he wrote his scripts, directed their production, and even gathered around him a fixed company of actors and technicians, Bergman achieved a totality of control that had hitherto appeared only on occasion. Moreover, his films were often bleak in implication and elusive in manner. Nevertheless, they proved appealing to notable audiences in both Sweden and abroad at the same time that foreign films in general began to circulate internationally.

By the beginning of the sixties, several developments had changed the situation of world cinema. Many directors had emerged who insisted on being authors of their work and not simply mechanics executing corporate blueprints. Italian neorealism had established verisimilitude as the main goal of film and had posited that audiences could enjoy movies without being comforted by them. Most important, a new international audience had been formed. Originally distinct from the mass audience, it came to influence mass taste so that "sure-fire" formulas began to fail at the box office and, by the end of the decade, hard-eyed producers were willing to back profitable art as they had earlier backed profitable pabulum. No wonder, then, that the sixties marks the largest breakthrough in cinema since the silent film era.

But before we consider this breakthrough, we must remember, despite its impressiveness, that it represents only a small fraction of the enormous total output of films. Most filmmakers and most audiences will always remain incorrigibly devoted to movies as an essentially mindless diversion. However, especially in Italy and France, filmmakers with more serious commitments began to flourish.

Of the latter group, in Italy, the most important figure is Michelangelo Antonioni. Beginning his career as a director of documentaries about the lower class, Antonioni eventually broke with doctrinaire neorealism because of his greater interest in the bourgeoisie, whose problems are more personal than social. Thus he was forced to develop a technique for documenting internal states, which he achieved, thereby revolutionizing world cinema, in his 1959 film *L'Avventura (The Adventure)*. *L'Avventura* expresses insights into middle-class urban life that had long been familiar from both modern fiction and social commentary. It presents a world in which people seem incapable of any commitment and are thrown back on impersonal and spiritually frustrating sensations. The film broke new ground by introducing such deep pessimism into an art so popular as cinema, but it was far more important for its formal innovations.

Antonioni moved even farther from theater than the neorealists, who had structured their situations conventionally and had never ignored the audience's emotions. Instead, Antonioni adopted an almost clinical manner and dispensed with plot. The search for a missing girl, which gives his film its narrative content, is never resolved. What we are asked to follow is not the story but the behavior of the characters, which illustrates Antonioni's formulation of a world that is spiritually dead. Moreover, Antonioni never permits his characters to discuss their plight. Instead, abandoning editorial cuts, he allows his camera to follow them, expecting us to draw inferences from their deeds, their gestures, and their interaction with the background. For example, we learn what is bothering the hero when we see him overturn the ink bottle of a student who is drawing the facsimile of a baroque cathedral. Earlier in the film, we had been told that Sandro was once an architect; now we see how bitter he is at having abandoned his youthful purpose. Similarly, we infer from visual elements one of the film's central themes: modern culture has despoiled its heritage. The carabinieri to whom Sandro goes while searching for his fiancée have fabricated an office by setting up ugly wooden partitions in a splendid baroque palace; a milling crowd of sullen and lustful men is visually counterpointed by an orderly parade of choirboys. Throughout the sixties, Antonioni experimented with other visual means to represent his insights—particularly by making color symbolic in *Red Desert* and *Blow-up*—but *L'Avventura* established the crucial fact that visual signs can suggest complicated, inward meanings.

In France, the sixties contained two major pairs of directors (Bresson and Resnais, Truffaut and Godard), each including one finished talent and one influential innovator. The first pair are close to Antonioni in their emphasis on subjective states and spiritual or intellectual themes. Of the two directors, the more important is Robert Bresson. Like Antonioni, Bresson treats complicated themes in a nonrhetorical way, but he differs in his neglect of visual symbolism and he is even more resolutely antitheatrical. Like the neorealists, Bresson avoids professional actors, eloquent dialogue, or highly sophisticated, articulate characters. Rather he makes films, usually adapted from literature, in which the lives of ordinary people in ordinary surroundings are made to yield spiritual significance. This is done by a highly concentrated method which focuses our attention so unrelentingly that the slightest event becomes portentous.

Bresson's method reached new heights of intensity in the sixties, but it is most easily understood from his 1956 masterpiece *A Man Escaped*. This scrupulously realistic portrayal of a prison break dispenses with generic convention by asserting in its title that the incarcerated Resistance fighter, Fontaine, will flee his German captors. Bresson is interested not in what will happen but in the meaning of the process. By restricting his camera to the hero's field of vision and by recording external sounds as an imprisoned man might hear them, he locks us into the hero's isolation, thereby producing in us, the audience, almost as fierce a desire for freedom. Then, forcing us to follow every painful moment of the escape, Bresson makes us realize the contention of his subtitle ("The Wind Bloweth Where It Listeth"): some providential force controls even the meanest of man's successes. We live through Fontaine's dependence on luck.

Alain Resnais takes subjectivism even farther than Bresson, but unlike Bresson, whose themes are religious, Resnais is mainly interested in history. Unfortunately, whereas Bresson writes his own scripts, Resnais has joined forces with writers who have not provided him with subjects worthy of his brilliant editing. However, he remains important for having trained audiences to accept discontinuous construction, in which scenes are joined not because they are temporarily successive but because they are perceived in this order by a human mind. Just as Antonioni taught directors how to photograph a way of life, and Bresson taught them how to photograph intangible forces, Resnais has taught the means of photographing subjective time.

The second important pair of French directors are far less internal. The "new wave," of which they are the most prominent exponents, prefers to emphasize the randomness and complexity of the external world, the resistance it offers to generalizations. The more successful of the two, François Truffaut, constructs his films through deliberate opposition of scenes with opposite emotional effects, as his masterpiece *Jules and Jim* makes clear. Here a dazzling variety of camera -techniques, tempos of performance, and editing are employed to make the spectator feel how mercurial is the central character, Catherine. She, in turn, exemplifies the mysteriousness of woman, who is as attractive as she is baffling. Thus, we get the following typical succession: Catherine, dressed like Chaplin's "The Kid," enters Jim's room, and the two men agree to accompany her to the street where she will test her new disguise. Presented through gay music and fast editing, the trio passes through a successful test and arrives at a foot bridge, where Catherine unexpectedly suggests a race. All agree, but Catherine bolts ahead while both men assume the starting position. Then the camera tracks alongside Catherine's head as the gay music is replaced on the soundtrack by the sound of her breathing. Thus, a delightful example of Catherine's love of sports modulates into a portentous example of her passionate desire for dominance; but the gaiety is immediately resumed before we can measure the full danger of the portent. And so it goes right through the end of the film, where a shot of Jules and Catherine being cremated is followed by Jim whistling his way down a garden path, relieved at having escaped the whirlpool into which his lover drew his best friend.

Like Truffaut, Jean-Luc Godard also constructs a cinema of surprise, in which, as in Truffaut's *Shoot the Piano Player,* farce turns into romantic tragedy and from that into gangster melodrama and back again, dizzying the audience but somehow reconciling it, through delight, to the contradictions of reality. However, Godard deplores reconciliation; in his films, the bafflement is rarely assuaged. Because his anarchical methods of plotting and editing are even more original than those of Antonioni, Bresson, Resnais, or Truffaut, Godard is almost surely the most influential filmmaker of his generation, the man who has most freed film from the need to tell well-constructed, unambiguous stories. But Godard's penchant for dispensing with all kinds of order makes his work often seem willful and chaotic. As Robert Frost said about free verse, Godard's style is a case of playing tennis without a net. Therefore, he is less important for his films than for the impulse they have given others to break away from formulas.

The period's other established directors are either without artistic novelty or they have become mired in ground which they had previously broken. Satyajit Ray, the excellent Indian director, essentially reproduces, on film, nineteenth-century social panoramas, as in his Apu trilogy or in the Chekovian *Music Room* (a sort of Hindu *Cherry Orchard*). Honorably avoiding easy appeal, his films document local culture at a pace that suggests real life; but they are artistically distinctive only for India, the rest of whose films are among the world's most escapist and trashy. The same may be said of Akira Kurosawa, although Japan has always had a number of serious directors, many of whom come close to rivaling him. Like certain Americans, Kurosawa has tried his hand at a wide variety of films, producing outstanding work in each category (particularly in action films, through his sumptuous recollections of the age of the samurai), but he cannot be associated with any single mode, whether of form or idea.

The Spaniard Luis Buñuel and the Italian Federico Fellini are the decade's chief examples of how the mighty can fall.

Buñuel began his career in silent film, where, with the help of artists like Salvador Dali, he taught the form how to deal with nonliteral reality, particularly dreams. In his recent sound films, however, he has fallen to obsessive presentation of what seem personal fantasies. Admirers may point to his courageous treatment of sexual drives and they enjoy his blasphemous anticlericalism, but his points are often conveyed through facile shocks, as in the famous parody of the Last Supper (in *Viridiana*), and his mastery of technique—particularly in his direction of actors—seems questionable.

Fellini also dwells on man's fantasy life. In the fifties, he satirized certain mass dreams both perceptively and with great wit (particularly in *The White Sheik* and *I Vitelloni*). In the sixties, however, Fellini himself seemed to have developed a carnival mentality that delights in the very sensationalism and sham opulence that have always characterized popular cinema. By seeming to disapprove of these effects, Fellini has maintained his reputation as a serious director, but films like *La Dolce Vita* and *Fellini Satyricon* make it difficult to distinguish satire from prurience. Nevertheless, Fellini produced one major work in this period: *8½*, which invents an engaging method for directorial autobiography.

So much cannot be said for Alfred Hitchcock, the master of cinematic suspense, who, in the sixties, had so lost his touch that he needed to resort to blatant sadism in order to achieve his ends. Before *Psycho,* Hitchcock had known how to evoke emotion simply through juxtaposition of images; now he must hold up a butcher knife. Despite its low artistic value, however, *Psycho* is historically important for having ushered in a new wave of blood.

The only major talent who did not arrive in the sixties but nonetheless managed to replenish himself during this decade is the always astonishing Bergman. During the fifties, Bergman made some brilliant films, but he did not add to the cinematic vocabulary. Indeed, notable works like *Wild Strawberries* and *The Magician* borrow freely from Buñuel. In the sixties, however, Bergman began to experiment with a type of film in which spectacle is avoided and the camera is used to explore the human face. The masterpiece of this mode is

Persona, but the earlier *Winter Light* is a more accessible example.

In the fifties, Bergman began to aspire toward ultimate themes (man's relationship with God and the consequent meaning of human life), but he tended to impose them on the action. By selecting a priest, professionally concerned with such questions, as the hero of *Winter Light,* Bergman went far in the direction of natural dramatization. Then by restricting the story to a single day and an intense series of confrontations between the priest and some parishoners, including his mistress, Bergman attained something of the intensity one finds in Bresson. His major accomplishment, however, was the long soliloquy—actually a letter read by the mistress to the priest—in which the brilliant acting of Ingrid Thulin, whose face Bergman held in relentless close-up, says more about the loneliness of man in a world without ultimate belief than scenes in which the issue is explicitly discussed.

The rest of the sixties was devoted to new talents working in old modes, the most fruitful of which remains neorealism. Especially in Italy, this continues to be the dominant style, though several younger directors have modified it almost out of recognition. Most orthodox of the new generation is Ermanno Olmi who, like Antonioni before him, began his career as a director of documentaries and later became interested in the middle class. But his present reputation rests on his second and third feature films, *The Sound of Trumpets* (*Il Posto*) and *The Fiancés.* Both employ nonprofessional actors and depict mundane events, but whereas De Sica might have emphasized the social problems exemplified in these stories, Olmi tries simply to document the truth, without polemical implication.

The Sound of Trumpets scrupulously follows a Milanese youth as he applies for a job, romances a fellow worker, and eventually moves up through the hierarchy to that menial post which is his probable destiny. Conveying both the poignance and the humor of his hero's life, Olmi's film recalls Truffaut. Moreover, it leavens its naturalist documentary with

Felliniesque caricature (during a farcical test given the applicants) and romantic lyricism (while the protagonists walk through the city). The ending particularly recalls Truffaut (the freeze shot in *The 400 Blows*) when the camera holds on the hero's face as a mimeograph machine, relentlessly turning, sounds the fixed condition of his life.

If *The Sound of Trumpets* recalls Truffaut, *The Fiancés* recalls Resnais. Though it recounts a typically neorealist experience (of a factory worker separated from his fiancée by a well-paying job in Sicily), *The Fiancés* is edited so as to capture not the social ambience but the consciousness of each principal character. This distinction is no mere adornment, for Olmi wishes to show that social forces don't operate by themselves. Rather, when the fiancés discover that separation permits an intimacy neither ever felt, we learn that their impoverishment is not financial.

With *The Fiancés,* Olmi effectively turns neorealism against the neorealist view of human behavior. Pier Paolo Pasolini, Bernardo Bertolucci, and Marco Bellocchio further modify the style. Originally a novelist and poet, Pasolini began his film career rather timidly with a derivative study of a lower-class thug (*Accatone*). Several years later, however, he applied neorealist technique to the Bible. Never altering the gospel of Saint Matthew but only illustrating it with lifelike scenes, Pasolini brilliantly drew from the text a proto-Marxian significance that fully accords with his own sympathies. Among the most visually stunning films ever made, *The Gospel According to Saint Matthew* is also inspiring in its evidence that the camera can interpret classic works. Subsequently, Pasolini has alternated between naturalist rereadings of classics, like *Oedipus Rex,* and fabricated modern stories on which he tries to impose some archetypal significance. Unfortunately, his later attempts fail; when, as in *Teorema,* he tries to incarnate God, he ludicrously does so by means of a young man's crotch. However, in a film like *Pigsty,* which intercuts a speechless tale of medieval cannibalism with a wittily rhetorical look at the aftermath of Naziism, Pasolini shows himself a resourceful innovator who uses cinematic technique to erase the boundaries that separate present and past.

Of the two younger men, Bellocchio is the more interesting. His second film, *China Is Near,* combines neorealist social documentary, theatrical intrigue, and Godardian shock. Introducing its principal characters through a series of brief scenes designed to confuse us, the film eventually explains not only the characters but also their relationship to Italian culture and politics. Because the most important characters are a pair of proletarian lovers and two aristocratic siblings, the story illustrates patterns of class conflict dear to the neorealist heart. But, following Godard, Bellocchio unveils his characters in ways that seem bizzare. For example, when the haughty countess orders her brother to expel the interlopers, she also announces her determination to take an inventory of her possessions so as to make sure that she and her brother have not been robbed. Then we see them compiling a list of books in their library, a task which, in its comic irrelevance, demonstrates both the pettiness of their power and their utter inability to protect it. No neorealist would make such a serious point through action so seemingly absurd, but Bellocchio dares this and much more. By disciplining his fancy with social accuracy, however, he produces a film whose surprises are never self-indulgent.

Outside Italy, realism has revitalized film in England and Eastern Europe. Theatricalism even more unqualified than that found in early French cinema has always been the bane of the English. For that reason, England was known mainly for her actors. But in the late fifties and early sixties, a group of "angry young men" began to do for English cinema what the "new wave" had done for the French: open film to contemporary life. As in Italy, films were made about the lower classes, but professional actors were employed (though they were deliberately less polished than the Oliviers and the Redgraves) and dialogue remained literary, though seasoned by argot. But the initial excitement caused by directors like Tony Richardson and Lindsay Anderson seems finally of merely local interest. The attitudinizing of Richardson's later films could have been discerned even in a seemingly naturalistic work like *The Loneliness of the Long Distance Runner*. Only Anderson seems to have maintained his original documentary intention, and his second film, *If . . .* , has earned him an even larger following than *This Sporting Life*. Nevertheless, though Anderson's subjects are "anti-Establishment," his emphatic staging and editing are even more overwrought than the antique style he professes to overturn. English cinema remains the least important of any produced in major European countries.

Far more interesting are the films coming from Eastern Europe. In Hungary, Czechoslovakia, and Poland, a generation trained in state film schools has begun applying incredible expertise to a newly candid confrontation with daily life. Greatest of these directors is the Pole Andrzej Wajda, though he flourished mainly in the fifties, when he did for the war and its aftermath what De Sica had done in Italy. During the sixties, however, Wajda did make one good film, in which he introduced a second important talent.

Innocent Sorcerers wittily documents a generation too "cool" for love. The hero, laid open to our inspection in the nearly wordless opening sequence, is a westernized devotee of jazz, gadgets, and his own invulnerability. He picks up a charming young lady at a night club, and they spend the evening together. But their sophistication allows them only to match wits. Appropriately, we often see them on either side of an electric wire, emblem of that life-style, newly problematic in Poland, which keeps them from falling in love. Filmed with great alertness to telling details, *Innocent Sorcerers* is also various in tone.

The coauthor of the script is Jerzy Skolimowski, who is to contemporary Eastern European cinema what Bellocchio and Bertolucci are to contemporary Italian. Like them, he has forged a technique, compounded of realism and Godard, that permits nonprogrammatic observation. His first movie, which he directed, wrote, and starred in, is an engagingly casual documentation of feckless Communist youth, unable to subscribe to the socialist pieties of a previous generation but also poignant in their frail imitation of Western affluence. After *Identification Marks: None,* however, Skolimowski seems to have taken to the virus rather than the freedom of Godard.

Roman Polanski, on the other hand, has been corrupted by commercialism. After a series of short, nearly surrealist films, Polanski directed the brilliant *Knife in the Water.* Whereas a film about a high school dropout was revolutionary in England, in Poland revolution meant ignoring factory workers for this tight little study of sexual tensions between an older married man and the young stud who threatens his dominance. Brilliant in its revelation of character through gesture, *Knife in the Water* is also suspensefully edited. This latter quality was instantly remarked in the West, which beckoned Polanski down the path that led through France and the purposeless mastery of *Repulsion* to America and the vulgar, even inept Hitchcockery of *Rosemary's Baby.*

Like some Slavic ballet dancers, certain Eastern European directors have defected to more liberal countries; but the dancers enter a world that insists on discipline, whereas the directors do not. The most prominent holdout in the younger generation is the Hungarian Miklós Jancsó, who choreographs studies of martial brutality to great effect (his most highly regarded films are *The Round-up, Silence and Cry,* and *The Red and the White*).

While most of the major Western European countries continue to achieve film art through realism, France once more shows that its directors prefer art to life. When they wanted models, men of the previous generation looked back toward classical French theater; their successors imitate American gangster novels. As Truffaut says, it is interesting to join French analysis of sentiments with the formulas of American action stories, and in a film like his *Shoot the Piano Player,* the combination works. But in a movie like Truffaut's *Mississippi Mermaid,* the analysis floats on the surface, failing to redeem the basic material from banality.

At the job of enriching Hollywood formulas, Claude Chabrol doesn't match Truffaut even at the latter's worst, but he is so cunning a technician that he warrants some notice. Master of understatement, Chabrol shows, in a film like *La Femme Infidele,* that artificial characters and plots can be

107

made to seem natural. However, as in all French films of this type, the allusions to American models—mostly Hitchcock—produced an effect that may rightfully be called academic.

Philippe De Broca, who began as an assistant to both compatriots, seems more original than Chabrol and the later Truffaut; instead, he has simply chosen livelier models to imitate. In his first three films, De Broca recalls René Clair's talent for visual humor and guileless flamboyance. Thus, in *The Joker,* the love-smitten hero, propelled by joy, breaks into a perfect imitation of Gene Kelly that is funny for being so openly outrageous. From Jean Vigo, De Broca learned the style of bittersweet lyricism. All of De Broca's important films move at the very end into a somberness of which we have heard faint rumors but which nevertheless strikes us with the force of surprise. Lately, however, De Broca has followed his fellow "new wave" directors down the path of increasingly tiresome imitations of cheap American genre films.

Although France produced some of the top filmmakers of the sixties, it has recently lost the predominance it shared with Italy. Perhaps as a result, serious filmgoers now range more widely in their search for important talent, and countries that scarcely mattered are now getting considerable attention. After the silent period, German film had seemed negligible; but lately, characteristic German mysticism and symbolic fantasy have been revived through the work of Jean-Marie Straub and Alexander Kluge, among others, thus attracting new interest in this country. As in literature, Latin America has made a sudden impact on the world in cinema, especially through the Brazilian *Cinema Nuevo* movement and the director Glauber Rocha. During the sixties, Sweden earned notoriety for *I Am Curious,* but it also produced, in the young writer-director-photographer-editor Jan Troell, a talent of the first magnitude. Naturalistic where Bergman is expressionistic, fluent and open where Bergman is knotted and hermetic, Troell (*Eeeny Meeny Miny Moe, Here Is Your Life*) is the first Swedish director who can be mentioned in the same breath as his great predecessor. However, renaissance was common in the sixties: in Henning Carlsen's *Hunger,* Denmark with Swedish collaboration has produced its greatest work since the silent films of Dreyer; and signs of life have appeared even where one had not previously looked, as in Senegal, of all places, with Ousmane Sembene.

On the other hand, publicized revitalization of American film is partly specious. When the studio system collapsed in the late fifties, artists were freed from corporate timidity, tyrannical formulas, and fear of recording the actual present. The result has been a series of films more faithful to contemporary manners than the normal Hollywood product. But the fidelity is only skin-deep.

In effect, America invented the art of motion pictures. By common consent, Charlie Chaplin was cinema's first great artist; even later, when Hollywood lost contact with the real world, American films maintained a verve that inspired other filmmakers. But America's system of production and distribution militated against serious talent. In the silent era, Chaplin could thrive because his most characteristic films were set in a timeless realm of *commedia dell'arte.* D. W. Griffith, on the other hand, had problems that were not only the result of his opulent projects; and Erich Von Stroheim, who was perhaps the greatest of our silent film directors, was relentlessly obstructed. The career of Orson Welles has become emblematic of American films, in its presentation of a man brought down largely by the studio system that interfered with basic artistic prerogatives. Nothing so demonstrates the nature of Hollywood as the unique success there of Alfred Hitchcock. A master technician, Hitchcock was allowed to go on making his terror machines, as he has, until the fuel ran out. Since his films bore little relation to the real world, he never threatened the manifold taboos and timidities that dominated men in the front office.

But as the front office began to make the wrong decisions, it began to be taken over by the director and his friends. American filmmakers had always been formidable craftsmen, even when they lacked serious purpose, because they possessed enormous technical resources. Now these resources could be put to uses beyond those of entertainment. In this, as in other ways, *Dr. Strangelove* is the key film of the sixties. Other countries could have made this delightful parody of the war machine, but no other country could have simulated the machine with such shocking plausibility. The sets for Kubrick's film (an unbearably complex airplane instrument panel, a vastly empty war room) are fundamental to its point. Moreover, the point and the attitude taken toward it are revolutionary in Hollywood: *Dr. Strangelove, mirabile dictu,* implies that human life is insane. The cheerful nihilism of the film's terminal holocaust was actually a creative moment in American films. Brilliantly acted, wittily scripted, and directed by a man who always knows when to feature image and when to highlight word, *Dr. Strangelove* remains the masterpiece of American cinema in the sixties.

But this opinion is not widely shared. Prior to the sixties, American film criticism scarcely existed, comment on cinema being confined to reviews by uninstructed journalists. During the decade, however, the growing passion for cinema brought into prominence a group of writers that had formerly flourished in small film journals, where they had worked out an aesthetic loosely based on the writings of French critics associated with *Cahiers du Cinéma*. Rebelling against the theatricalism of their compatriots, the French turned toward American films for an antidote; but since American films were distinguished, if at all, for style (which was not interfered with by producers) rather than subject, such criticism mindlessly emphasized camera angles and staging as if meaning were an irrelevancy. Coinciding with a general attack on discursive reasoning, this brand of criticism has convinced a generation of viewers that the medium is the message, with the result that audiences who would rather not think anyway have received sanction for their laziness. Thus a film like *Dr. Strangelove* is regarded as old fashioned, because it eschews "mind-boggling effects," while Kubrick's later and cavernously empty *2001: A Space Odyssey* is regarded as "the ultimate trip."

More antagonistic to film art even than this emphasis on effectism is the new subtlety with which American film provides wish fulfillment. Notoriously escapist prior to the sixties,

American films used to sanctify the values of the middle class: success, happy marriage, material affluence. In the sixties, however, the middle-class audience started to stay home, where it could enjoy even more narcotizing lies on television, at even lower cost. Into the vacuum left by that defection rushed an audience of young people, which, having imbibed the new criticism, is more responsive to technical innovation than to maturity of feeling and comprehension. Sadly, this audience has proven no less susceptible to flattery than the generation which flocked to Clark Gable rather than Mike Nichols and cared more about the final clinch than the final freeze frame. As a result, the "new American film" may be new wine in new bottles, but it still has the stale old flavor.

The Graduate, Bonnie and Clyde, and *Easy Rider*—the most noted of these films—make the point. Each is more technically daring than its predecessors; each treats characters that would never have been featured on American screens; each is truer to contemporary manners than to the corporate image of what the audience would like to think of as contemporary manners. But each film plays to stock responses and reflects audience prejudices as shamelessly as the discredited old models.

The Graduate is the worst, and most profitable, example, because it grafts serious issues onto a rather old-fashioned farce about the foolish male virgin and the older woman. Moreover, it opts for the callow youngster for reasons that seem independent of his character in the film. Though rapacious, Mrs. Robinson is manifestly a more interesting person than Benjamin, who makes no strenuous effort to relate to her, despite his pretentions in that line, and who is as casual in his pursuit of an easy lay. But because Mrs. Robinson is adult (read: libidinous) whereas, when left to himself (as with her daughter), Benjamin is as pure as Andy Hardy, we are meant to hate the older woman while applauding the young man. So expected is the audience's narcissistic fixation on youthful innocence, that the writer and director can totally alter Mrs. Robinson's personality—changing her from a bored suburban matron into a veritable Medea—without fearing that they will be accused of inconsistency. What we witness in *The Graduate* is not an inspection of contemporary life but an apology for the young people caught in its net of affluence. That the affluence—insofar as it is portrayed— has also trapped the oldsters is to be forgotten. Rather the oldsters are illogically made into the evil force so as to permit melodramatic satisfaction. We are back with cops and robbers, only the villains carry sexual weapons and wear wrinkles rather than black hats, while the heroes are all Peter Pan in mod attire.

In *Bonnie and Clyde,* the cops and robbers are literal, but the latter are portrayed as crypto-revolutionaries against a society in the throes of economic collapse, harmful mainly to the poor. The cops, on the other hand, are all imbecile sadists who submit the heroes to an overkill familiar from American foreign policy. These hints were not lost on an audience that might otherwise have been repelled by the film's extreme violence. However, when violence is represented as the obscenity of "them" against "us" it becomes subtly affirmative.

Easy Rider is more engaging than the other films because it does contain an occasional scene of incisive social observation (like the one in which a lunchroom of rednecks is driven to homicidal rage by the sight of men with long hair). But this movie even more clearly indicates the virus that threatened to cripple American cinema just as it was about to walk in adult fashion. More arbitrarily even than *The Graduate* and *Bonnie and Clyde, Easy Rider* implies that young and loose are *ipso facto* superior to old and established, and it panders even more operatically to youthful paranoia. One could easily have predicted that its success would have signalled the flood of testimonials to youth in which American film is currently drowning.

This is particularly disturbing because the aging of men of genius, coupled with a worldwide economic crisis, has forced a decline in foreign film at the same time that the American revival threatens to abort itself. Giants like Antonioni descend to the lowest point of their careers on the American mainland (*Zabriskie Point*); men like Truffaut become increasingly mired in private trickery. Meanwhile any

112

moderately imaginative young man with a camera can achieve effects previously reserved to genius and can find some producer to back him so long as he does not affront the prejudices of the new audience. To the latter, content becomes increasingly irrelevant while technique—increasingly resourceful—becomes the *dernier cri*. While the young flock to gewgaws and lies, the old flock to skin flicks, which mock the realist imperative by being truthful only to man's genitals and then only so far as the cops will allow. The new frontier of truth has dwindled to the dimensions of a dangling penis.

But the current diminishment of film art is not irreversible. If few new geniuses seem to be striding into the seventies, it is obviously too early to signal the end of an epoch. An unprecedentedly large number of countries are producing serious directors. Moreover, as Bergman has shown, established talent can renew itself. Young Americans may tire of flattering fables even more quickly than their elders tire of pornography. Still, we must remember that cinema is incomparably more dependent than other arts on the taste of its audience. Unless he pleases some segment of the public, no director can find backing for his work. For this reason, teachers, critics, and film librarians share an important responsibility. To the extent that we help ourselves and others to distinguish between films that provide truthful representation of our humanity and those which divert us from this task (however diverting they may be), and to the extent that we educate ourselves and others in that repertory on which sound taste is founded, we will help film to be not only "the art of now" but also an art in the future.

Selected Filmography

Since I have not seen every sixties' film with claims to artistic excellence, let alone every film in this period, the following list is incomplete. It is meant to include, however, every director of importance who flourished in the sixties, many of the outstanding films, and several films which, despite flaws, broke important ground (e.g., *Last Year at Marienbad*). Occasionally (as with *Easy Rider* and *The Grad-*

113

uate), I include films that are more important as cultural manifestations than as art. Each entry includes the scenarist (sc.) and photographer (ph.) and, where contributions are especially important, names of editors (ed.), composers (mus.), and costume and set designers (c.&s.). Principal actors (act.) are listed except in cases where the director employed amateurs or actors who have no reputation outside their native country.

ANDERSON, LINDSAY
If . . . (sc. David Sherwin; ph. Miroslav Ondricek; ed. David Gladwell).

ANTONIONI, MICHELANGELO
Blow-up (sc. Antonioni, Tonino Guerra, Edward Bond; ph. Carlo di Palma; act. Vanessa Redgrave, David Hemmings).

Eclipse (sc. Antonioni, Guerra, Elio Bartolini, Ottiero Ottieri; ph. Gianni di Venanzo; ed. Eraldo da Roma; act. Monica Vitti, Alain Delon).

Red Desert (sc. Antonioni, Guerra; ph. di Palma; ed. da Roma; act. Vitti, Richard Harris).

L'Avventura (sc. Antonioni, Bartolini, Guerra; ph. Aldo Scavarda; ed. da Roma; mus. Giovanni Fusco; act. Vitti, Gabriele Ferzetti).

La Notte (sc. Antonioni, Guerra, Ennio Flaiano; ph. di Venanzo; act. Vitti, Jeanne Moreau, Marcello Mastroianni).

BELLOCCHIO, MARCO
China Is Near (sc. Bellocchio, Elda Tattoli; ph. Tonino Delli Colli).

BERGMAN, INGMAR
Persona (sc. Bergman; ph. Sven Nykvist; act. Bibi Andersson, Liv Ullmann).

Shame (sc. Bergman; ph. Nykvist; act. Ullmann, Max von Sydow, Gunnar Bjornstrand).

The Silence (sc. Bergman; ph. Nykvist; act. Ingrid Thulin, Gunnel Lindbloom).

Winter Light (sc. Bergman; ph. Nykvist; act. Bjornstrand, Thulin).

BERTOLUCCI, BERNARDO
Before the Revolution (sc. Bertolucci; ph. Aldo Scavarda).

BRESSON, ROBERT
Une Femme Douce (sc. Bresson; ph. Ghislain Cloquet; act. Dominique Sanda).
Au Hasard Balthazar (sc. Bresson; ph. Cloquet; act. Anne Wiazemsky).
Mouchette (sc. Bresson; ph. Cloquet).

BUÑUEL, LUIS
Belle de Jour (sc. Buñuel, Jean-Claude Carriere; ph. Sacha Vierny; act. Catherine Deneuve, Michel Piccoli).
Simon of the Desert (sc. Buñuel; ph. Gabriel Figueroa; act. Sylvia Pinal).
Viridiana (sc. Buñuel, Julio Alejandro; ph. Jose Aguayo; act. Pinal, Francisco Rabal).

CARLSEN, HENNING
Hunger, (sc. Carlsen, Peter Seeberg; ph. Henning Kristiansen; act. Per Oscarsson, Gunnel Lindblom).

CHABROL, CLAUDE
La Femme Infidele (sc. Chabrol; ph. Jean Rabier; ed. Jacques Gaillard; act. Stephanie Audran, Michel Bouquet, Maurice Ronet).

DE BROCA, PHILIPPE
The Five Day Lover (sc. de Broca, Daniel Boulanger; ph. Jean Penzer; mus. Georges Delerue; act. Jean-Pierre Cassel, Jean Seberg, Micheline Presle).
The Joker (sc. Boulanger; ph. Pierre L'Homme; mus. Delerue; act. Cassel, Genevieve Cluny, Anouk Aimée).
The Love Game (sc. de Broca, Boulanger; ph. Penzer; mus. Delerue; act. Cluny, Cassel).

DE SETA, VITTORIO
The Bandits of Orgosolo (sc. & ph. De Seta).

FELLINI, FEDERICO
8½ (sc. Fellini, Tullio Pinelli, Ennio Flaiano, Brunella Rondi; ph. Gianni di Venanzo; mus. Nino Rota; c. & s. Piero

Gherardi; act. Marcello Mastroianni, Anouk Aimée, Sandra Milo).

La Dolce Vita (sc. Fellini, Flaiano, Pinelli, Rondi; ph. Otello Martelli; mus. Rota; c. & s. Gherardi; act. Mastroianni, Aimée, Anita Ekberg, Alain Cuny).

GODARD, JEAN-LUC

Breathless (sc. Godard; ph. Raoul Coutard; act. Jean Seberg, Jean-Paul Belmondo).

My Life to Live (sc. Godard; ph. Coutard; mus. Michel Legrand; act. Anna Karina).

Weekend (sc. Godard; ph. Coutard; mus. Albert Duhamel).

HEIFETZ, JOSEPH

The Lady with the Dog (sc. Heifetz; ph. Andrei Moskvin, Dmitri Meshkiev).

HITCHCOCK, ALFRED

Psycho (sc. Joseph Stefano; ph. John L. Russell; act. Anthony Perkins, Janet Leigh).

HOPPER, DENNIS

Easy Rider (sc. Hopper, Peter Fonda, Terry Southern; ph. Laszlo Kovacs; act. Hopper, Fonda, Jack Nicholson).

JANCSÓ, MIKLOS

Silence and Cry (sc. Jancsó, Gyula Hernadi; ph. Janos Kende).

The Red and the White (sc. Jancsó, Hernadi, Georgi Mdivani; ph. Tomas Somlo).

The Round-up (sc. Hernadi; ph. Somlo).

JESSUA, ALAIN

Life Upside Down (sc. Jessua; ph. Jacques Robin; act. Charles Denner).

KUBRICK, STANLEY

Dr. Strangelove (sc. Kubrick, Terry Southern, Peter George; ph. Gilbert Taylor; act. Peter Sellers, George C. Scott, Sterling Hayden, Keenan Wynn).

KUROSAWA, AKIRA
Yojimbo (sc. Kurosawa, Ryuzo Kikushima; ph. Kazuo Miyagawa; act. Toshiro Mifune).

LOSEY, JOSEPH
The Servant (sc. Harold Pinter; ph. Douglas Slocombe; act. Dirk Bogarde, James Fox, Sarah Miles).

NICHOLS, MIKE
The Graduate (sc. Calder Willingham, Buck Henry; ph. Robert Surtees; mus. Paul Simon; act. Anne Bancroft, Dustin Hoffman).

OLMI, ERMANNO
The Fiancés (sc. Olmi; ph. Lamberto Caimi).
The Sound of Trumpets (*Il Posto*) (sc. Olmi; ph. Caimi).

PASOLINI, PIER PAOLO
Pigsty (sc. Pasolini; ph. Tonino Delli Colli; act. Pierre Clementi, Jean-Pierre Leaud, Ugo Tognazzi, Anne Wiazemsky).
The Gospel According to Saint Matthew (ph. Tonino Delli Colli).

PENN, ARTHUR
Bonnie and Clyde (sc. Robert Benton, David Newman; ph. Burnett Guffey; ed. Dede Allen; act. Warren Beatty, Faye Dunaway, Michael J. Pollard, Gene Hackman, Estelle Parsons).

POLANSKI, ROMAN
Knife in the Water (sc. Polanski, Jerzy Skolimowski, Jakub Goldberg; ph. Halina Prugar).

PONTECORVO, GILLO
The Battle of Algiers (sc. Franco Solinas; ph. Marcello Gatti).

RAY, SATYAJIT
The Music Room (sc. Ray; ph. Subrata Mitra).

RESNAIS, ALAIN
Last Year at Marienbad (sc. Alain Robbe-Grillet; ph. Sacha Vierny; act. Delphine Seyrig, Giorgio Albertazzi).

ROSI, FRANCESCO

Salvatore Giuliano (sc. Rosi, Enzo Provenzale, Suso Cecchi D'Amico, Franco Solinas; ph. Gianni di Venanzo).

SKOLIMOWSKI, JERZY

Identification Marks: None (sc. Skolimowski; ph. Witold Mickiewicz; act. Skolimowski).

TROELL, JAN

Eeny Meeny Miny Moe (sc. Troell, Bengt Forslund, Clas Engstrom; ph. Troell; act. Per Oscarsson).

Here Is Your Life (sc. Troell, Forslund; ph. Troell).

TRUFFAUT, FRANÇOIS

Jules and Jim (sc. Truffaut, Jean Gruault; ph. Raoul Coutard; mus. Georges Delerue; act. Jeanne Moreau, Oskar Werner, Henri Serre).

Shoot the Piano Player (sc. Truffaut, Marcel Moussy; ph. Coutard; mus. Delerue; act. Charles Aznavour, Nicole Berger).

The Bride Wore Black (sc. Truffaut, Jean-Louis Richard; ph. Coutard; mus. Bernard Herrmann; act. Moreau, Jean-Claude Brialy, Charles Denner, Michel Bouquet).

The Four Hundred Blows (sc. Truffaut, Moussy; ph. Henri Decae; mus. Jean Constantine; act. Jean-Pierre Leaud).

WAJDA, ANDRZEJ

Innocent Sorcerers (sc. Jerzy Andrzejewski, Jerzy Skolimowski; ph. Krzysztof Winiewicz).

ANIMA RISING:

LITTLE MAGAZINES
IN THE SIXTIES

Len Fulton

The little magazines and small presses of the decade affected and were affected by all the major social issues of the
time: peace and war, race, education, censorship, underground papers; and later in the decade: ecology, Indian
rights, Women's and Gay Liberation, and so forth. An even
slightly informative discussion of the entire spectrum of
forces running into the small print media would take much
more (I hope recycled) paper than I have here been issued.
But it is my belief that the general frontal pressure of small
presses in the sixties was created by the emerging action ethic
of youth, which evolved quickly into a do-it-yourself praxis
and a search for generational identity. Then, there were three
more particular influences which I'll take up at length, one
technological and economic (offset printing), one aesthetic
(concrete poetry), and one spiritual (mimeography). True to
the thirst for wholeness and relatedness that pervaded the
decade, these influences remain inseparable except under the

Len Fulton, a small press publisher (Dustbooks), is chairman of
the directors of the 250-member committee of Small Magazines Editors and Publishers (COSMEP).

most academic analysis, rolling together in an incessantly overlapping and altering pattern. And other influences are as well strung into the current: freedom of language and the belief that it belongs to the person using it; the proliferation of *book* publishing; poetry pamphleteering by the small periodicals to a point of blurring the distinction between book and magazine (*The Outsider* is called a "book periodical," for example), and the eventual interchangeability of the terms "little magazine" and "small press," just one manifestation of the liquidizing (not liquidating) of traditional boundaries between genres and media, and a redefinition in *process* rather than structure; an alienation from the austere and isolated scholarship of the university—or any austere and isolated scholarship—or any austere and isolated *anything*—and an increasing suspicion of university or institutional sponsorship or of those publications so sponsored; the falling into general disrepute of the old "school" phenomenon which made the critic's life so easy and smart; the appearance of definite if sometimes evanescent regional influences; the indurate poetry of Charles Bukowski; and the organization of the small presses in 1968 into the Committee of Small Magazine Editors and Publishers (COSMEP). The decade with which I am really concerned here is not in fact a ten-year period at all, but more like four or five years, starting in 1963 and 1964 with the sudden inception of so many important small presses, and coinciding incidentally with the inception of the first underground newspapers. Nevertheless, some of the immediate forerunners of the small presses of this time in the United States were Tuli Kupferberg's *Birth* (started in 1957 and carried well into the decade as *Birth Press*); Ed Sanders' *Fuck You/A Magazine of the Arts*; Robert Bly's *The Fifties* (started in 1958, changed to *The Sixties* and now *The Seventies*); LeRoi Jones' *Yugen* (1958–62); and John Bryan's *Renaissance* (1961).

Although the form of printing known as "planographic" (flat surface) can be traced back to Germany in 1796, it was not until photoengraving methods were developed in letterpress printing that the offset process became a reality. In 1904 a lithographer in New Jersey named Ira W. Rubel came upon the modern offset process through an error of his press feeder. He discovered that to run the image from its original cylinder onto a rubber blanket and thence to the paper greatly increased clarity of the printing. The process was used and developed up into the fifties but, because of expensive investments in letterpress machinery, the big newspapers and periodicals did not convert to offset. There were no offset presses on the magnitude of the giant, web-fed letterpress machines, and no typesetting or accessory equipment equal to the Linotype machine, the Ludlow typecaster, and so on. As far as I know the first offset daily newspaper in the United States was the *Middletown* (N.Y.) *Daily Record* (1956), which had to have its press custom built. There followed, apparently, the production of larger offset equipment, which had the effect of throwing the smaller, used machinery onto the market. As advances were made quickly in the technology of first-line items, these used presses became more plentiful, cheaper, and better. They began to land in garages, cellars, and front parlors.

The conversion from letterpress to offset printing in the sixties by the small presses is statistical fact. The proliferation of these presses early in the decade is the basic technical stimulus to the entire small and underground press movement. Table 1 and figure 1 show the unremitting ten-year trend: In 1960 some 78 percent of little magazines were letterpress printed, 17 percent were offset; by 1969 only 31 percent were letterpress, 54 percent were offset.

Table 1. Magazines by Year and Printing Process; 1960, 1965—69

Year	Percent of Total			Number of Magazines in Sample
	Letterpress	Offset	Mimeo	
1960	78	17	5	311
1965	46	31	23	230
1966	44	34	22	426
1967	42	38	20	593
1968	35	45	20	465
1969	31	54	15	487

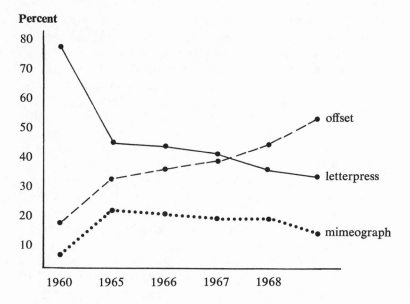

Figure 1. Changes in printing process in the small presses, 1960—68.

SOURCES:
Directory of Little Magazine and Small Presses (Dustbooks, 1964–69)
The International Guide (*Trace*, 1959–60).

This process was made-to-order for the fluid, "do-it-your-self-*now*" current that began to engulf the sixties. It took no accessory equipment on the order of that required in letter-press, and the advent of direct platemaking and direct masters simplified things still more. Little space was required for storage and operation, and many smaller models could be moved by one man quickly and entirely. Most of all, how-ever, for the little magazines justified typesetting could be done for a nickel a line—or for just about nothing by the editor on his own typewriter. And if a given contributor's work went beyond the usual "straight matter" (prose or po-etry) toward visual art, it could be reproduced faithfully at little or no extra cost, and with little or no condescension to the intervening printing technology. This last of course is critical, for finally the experimenter and his editor (often one and the same) were wholly *free* in point of technological fact.

Freedom in that decade, as we know, was a thirst touched off by something far deeper and more universal than the coming of the print medium into proletarian hands (and things were happening in light and sound, too). Freedom was the midcentury *Zeitgeist,* with its taproot in the early-century failures of industrialization, the sundry dehumanizations that started with the First Great War and reached its most imposing moments over Hiroshima and Nagasaki. As always, that *Zeitgeist* expressed itself most exquisitely in the arts, and especially those arts with little "to lose" from the truth—the avant-garde, the experimental, the underground—the arts to which commercial viability was not a founding consideration. In the print media nothing stood readier as a vehicle than the little magazine.

The spiritual essence of the poetry that came to be known as "concrete" lay in the evolution of perception and theory in this century from static towards dynamic modes. The development of quantum physics and of behavioral and Gestalt psychologies early in the century are evidences of this in the sciences and humanities, whose premises are infinitely simpler than those of art. In the literate arts early moves toward Dadaism, surrealism, and later antirealism were in this direction, as were surrealism and abstract expressionism in painting and "atonality" and serialism in music. Expanded communications, increased mobility, and simply population growth itself contributed to a general sense of fluidity that blossomed after mid-century, which led inevitably to the notion that there was no one way to do anything, only many ways with varying probabilities of betterness. This relativeness led to exploration of intermediary areas (*energies* would be a term more in keeping with the spirit) and a seeming irreverence for old and static categories and terms. Much here is a tremendous if technologized re-turn toward what the styles of "primitive" man must have been. This thought is important, at least, in considering concrete poetry as it developed into the sixties in Europe as a virtual renaissance.

It began in the late forties and early fifties with the "ideograms" of Brazilian Decio Pignatari and Diter Rot of Iceland; and with the "constellations" of the Swiss Eugen Gomringer, whom the American Emmett Williams refers to in the foreword to his massive *An Anthology of Concrete Poetry* (Something Else Press, 1967) as "the acknowledged father" of it all. Gomringer and Pignatari met in 1955, and out of this meeting came plans for an anthology titled *Konkrete Poesie,* which was unfortunately not published. During the fifties similar and often independent work was being done by Haroldo de Campos of Brazil, Kitasono Katue of Japan, Ian Hamilton Finlay of Scotland, and Pierre Garnier of France. Essentially though, the early efforts in concrete poetry began on either of two continents, Europe or South America, and their convergence provided the nucleus for an international poetry Gomringer called "supranational." The ideogram was based on a visual syntax and an analogical method of composition rather than, as in traditional poetry, a grammatical syntax and a logical or discursive composition. The semantic elements in an ideogram cannot be separated from the visual elements. This latter is also a basic force in the Gomringer constellations. For Gomringer the poem was a functional object held in dynamic balance "as if it were drawing stars together to form a cluster." It would seem that the dynamic quality of the poem for Gomringer was slightly more critical than the visual presentation of an idea (as in the ideogram). The convergence then produced a poetry universally called "concrete," a term that only in the last year or two seems to have come to be less than descriptive of the work being done. Concrete is "a poetry far beyond paraphrase," says Emmett Williams, "a poetry that often asks to be completed or activated by the reader, a poetry of direct presentation—the *word, not words, words, words* or expressionistic squiggles—using . . . semantic, visual and phonetic elements of language as raw materials."

A number of small magazines published this work in the fifties. These included *Vou* (Tokyo), *Noigandres* (Edicoes Invencao, São Paulo), *Ideogramme* (Switzerland), *Bok* (Reykjavík), and *Bord-dikter* (Stockholm). This last published work by Oyvind Fahlstrom as early as 1952; and *Vou* was founded in 1935 as a Japanese avant-garde magazine. *Noi-gandres* was produced in the fifties by a group of Brazilian poets, of whom Haroldo de Campos was one of the most brilliant, emergent international figures.

In the sixties the concepts and arguments of the concrete poetry of Gomringer and Pignatari provided a departure point for a new revolution. Whereas these early concretists were interested in crossing the traditional boundaries between the literary and visual arts—itself a revolutionary proposition—those of the sixties moved out almost recklessly (and certainly courageously) in such flamboyant directions that virtually all art forms were effected. The revolution came to Great Britain, to Canada, and to the United States, though its main vanguard—at least as concerned its original inclinations—remained in continental Europe and South America.

The experiments in "word-plastics" of J. F. Bory, editor with Julien Blaine of *Approches* and with J. Gerz of *Agentzia* (both Paris), and of Ugo Carrega, editor of *Tool* (Milan), are outstanding. Bory uses word conglomerates and expanding, exploding characters to communicate feelings such as fear and ideas such as time. His work covers an enormous range—from such photographic experiments as *erotographie* (*Approches* 2) to the handprinted permutational Chinese script of *Bêche* (*Approches,* 1966), and *Whispering* (*Approches,* 1966) in which the voice volume implied for the words (in English) is rendered by light-to-lighter shades of yellow, with a typical expanding-contracting arrangement. The magazine carries work by Ilse and Pierre Garnier, editors of *Les Lettres* (Paris), whose concern is with spatialism and a supranational poetry (see "Pour Une Poesie Supranationale"), and includes an essay or spatialism, plus spatialist work by the Garniers, "Poemes mechaniques architectures" (in *Approches* 1), some plastic poems by Kitasono Katue of Japan, excellent collages by Claude Pelieu of the United States, and much else.

Ugo Carrega of *Tool* (Milan) is another brilliant artist in "the world of verbal-phonetic signs (of the words apart from their meaning or sound) and the world of graphic signs (their physical appearance, the 'matter' of the word on the page)." Carrega's work often takes on organic, map-like qualities (as in *non principio e fine* or the card set *mikrokosmos*) but can also be expansive and flamboyant like Bory's (as in *idea rotore* and *segno vita*). In *Tool,* a large and beautiful folio, Carrega has used work by Julien Blaine, Herman Damen, Luigi Ferro, and many others.

Other directions on the Continent have been sought by Martino Oberto, editor of *Ana Eccetera* (Genoa), who connects graphics, words, and their analogical equivalents and seeks "the operational awareness of the specific exercise of linguistic terms, integrative levels for a type of language programmed to philosophical abstractism." Daniela Palazzoli and Gianni-Emilio Simonetti, editors of *Da-a/u dela* (Milan), verge toward musical experiments such as Sylvano Bussotti's "The Rara Requiem" which, in all its complexity, fits on a 4½ by 10½ inch card; Carl Weissner, editor of *Klactoveedsedsteen* (Heidelberg), has published tape recorder mutations by William Burroughs, Claude-Pelieu, and himself and is interested in cut-up art, tape experiments, "word/sound bruitage."

In Great Britain one of the most important forces in this movement has been Ian Hamilton Finlay, a typographer and sometime toymaker, publisher of Wild Hawthorne Press and a concrete magazine called *Poor. Old. Tired. Horse.* He has worked in environmental poetry, sculpture poetry, glass poetry (his "wave/rock" as photographed by Patrick Eagar is well known), and a series of standing poems. He has divided his work into "fauve" and "suprematist" poems, apparently to distinguish between those which make reference to events outside themselves and those which are unified semantic and graphic forms. He has also published kinetic poems and a series of kinetic booklet poems. His 1960 book, *Glasgow Beasts, An A BurdHaw, An Inseks, An, Aw, A Fush,* caused an uproar among literary Scots.

Elsewhere in Great Britain, Cavan McCarthy devoted his mimeo mag, *Tlaloc,* to visual/concrete poems and to communication between, and information about, concretists throughout the world; John Furnival and Dom Sylvester Houedard of *Openings* published poster poems, graphic scores, cards, and folders of concrete poetry; John J. Sharkey, who with his wife Sonia edited *Loc* and *Lisn*, published "post-concrete" poetry—semiotics (code poetry introduced by Decio Pignatari and Luiz Angelo Pinto in 1964), computer poetry, nonverbal poetry, and spatial poetry. The poster and cartoon poetry of Christopher Logue has been outstanding.

South America has, of course, continued to be a place of great experiment and invention in concrete poetry throughout the sixties, as can be seen by the constant references in the preceding text. The founding of the Noigandres Group (1952) and the "pilot plan for concrete poetry" (1958) together with the work of such internationally brilliant poets as Haroldo de Campos, Augusto de Campos, and Decio Pignatari provided Brazil with as rich a heritage in the genre as any nation in the world. It was largely through proselytization by these Brazilians that concrete poetry came to the attention of such artists as Ian Hamilton Finlay of Scotland, Kitasono Katue of Japan, and Dom Sylvester Houedard of England; and it was these same Brazilians who suggested the term *concrete* to Eugen Gomringer in Switzerland in 1954, launching the international poetry. What is now a tradition continues, centered largely in São Paulo, Brazilia University, and Rio de Janeiro. The Argentine magazine *Diagonal Cero* (Buenos Aires), edited by Edgardo Antonio Vigo, has been highly influential in the South American and international concrete movement throughout the entire decade. The work of Vigo himself in stylish geometrical and punch poetry has pressed ever outward against any limits the genre possesses. *Diagonal Cero* is associated with Guillermo Deisler of Chile and Miguel Ángel Fernandez of Paraguay.

The Canadian movement in concrete poetry has rested largely in the hands of a multimedia Toronto group centered at Ganglia Press (*Gronk, Synapsis*) and Coach House Press. Work by bp Nichol, David Aylward, David Harris (also recently bylined "David uu"), Rah Smith, Bill Bissett, and Jon Riddell has appeared. A good example of this work is bp Nichol's *Journeying and the Returns* (1967), a package containing a book, a record, and assorted small pamphlets called "skoobs" by England's Cavan McCarthy, which is *books* spelled backward. The Toronto group has been interested in "concrete sound kinetic and related borderblur poetry," and has been allied both spiritually and materially with the Cleveland mimeo work of the late d. a. Levy, and that D. r. Wagner's *Runcible Spoon* (now in Sacramento, California).

In fact, any discussion of the concrete poetry movement in the United States beyond the extraordinary work of New York-based editors such as Emmett Williams and Dick Higgins of Something Else Press, or Jerome Rothenberg of *Some/things*—all essentially international in character and thrust—is rather inextricably bound to the mimeograph movement. One of the earliest and most courageous innovators was the young d. a. Levy (1942–68) of Cleveland to whom concrete poetry was only one of the possibilities open to a "poet-editorpublisher." This is an agglutination which Levy himself coined, and it more or less summarizes what Levy and much of American concrete was about. His very earliest concrete poetry (e.g., *Book #6*) was relatively free of manifest social and political reference; he experimented with stencil, ink, and color and with borderblur and other innovations of form. In all his work, early and late, concrete and otherwise, his preoccupation with mysticism and Zen philosophy inevitably emerged. *The Tibetan Stroboscope,* a newsprint collection published in 1968 at Ayizan Press, Cleveland, is notable for its mystical concrete/collage theme. Levy called it "an experiment in destructive writing, 'other' communications and concrete prose."

In the mid-sixties he ran afoul of the brutal and reactionary Cleveland constabulary which took a stereotypically narrow view of his *Marrahwannah Quarterly* and related activities. Before he knew it, Cleveland's youth had cast him in the role of martyr, which he eschewed with only limited success. Under constant harassment he refused to remain socially or aesthetically isolated, and so his work, concrete included, took on more and more social, political, and psychological implications. ("Visualized Prayer for the American God #6" is a good example, done in 1967) sometimes approaching cartoon art, and certainly spilling

into photo-collage and cut-up art, which he produced volumi-
nously.

Little truly American concrete poetry outside New York
City was uninfluenced, either in spirit or form, by d. a. Levy
and the work that emerged from Cleveland in the mid-sixties.
A case can be made, if sometimes tenuously, for lines of alli-
ance between Levy and the work published by Morris Edelson
of *Quixote* (Madison, Wisconsin), Douglas Blazek of *Olé*
(Bensonville, Illinois and Sacramento, California) and D. r.
Wagner of *Runcible Spoon* (Niagara Falls and Sacramento).
Wagner was in fact a close friend and publisher of Levy in
Cleveland in the early sixties, and published his *Cleveland:
Rectal Eye Visions* (1966), *Tomb Stone as a Lonely Charm*
(1967), and others.

One United States mimeo-concrete poet-publisher whose
work bears little of the Levy influence, however, is Wally
Depew, whose PN2 and PN3 series (Sacramento) is founded
in and influenced almost exclusively by word-plastics, chiefly
those of Bory and Blaine in France. Done in the late sixties
Depew's small (3½/4 inch) booklets—such as *Permutations,
The Alphabet Book, The Number Book,* and *Mechanical
Variations and Reversals*—all show an exacting intellectual
and technical thrust that is more in the spirit of the Europeans and Brazilians. (Compare Depew's latest book, *The
Purple R,* with Bory's *Bêche,* for example; or his *Pornbook*
with Bory's *erotographie* in *Approches* 2; or his *Punch Book*
with the elaborate geometric efforts of the Argentine magazine, *Diagonal Cero.*)

Oddly enough, however, these two lines of influence through
the sixties—d. a. Levy and the Europeans—seem to be con-
verging in Sacramento, California, as Wagner and Depew
begin to collaborate, *Runcible Spoon* having just published
Depew's *Bounce Poem* by Gestetner duplicator.

Other parties in the United States to the European concrete movement have been Aram Saroyan's *Lines* (N.Y.C.)
in 1964–65 and, since 1967, Jan Jacob Herman's *Earthquake*
(San Francisco), which has published work by William S.
Burroughs, Claude Pelieu, Carl Weissner, and J. F. Bory.

When the small magazine or press could not be a primary vehicle for this "new" poetry (as it could not, for example, with much intermedium art, "happenings," autocreative/destructive art, or environmental poetry such as glass poetry), it became an effective promoter and cataloger. Hence, *Something Else Newsletter* (N.Y.C.) was designed "to promote development of critical attitudes and concepts appropriate to Happenings and other avant garde works that fall in between conventional media." *Quixote* (Madison) has recorded theater and happening art pictorially. *Labris* (Antwerp) has articulated the tenets of "poejazz." *Klactoveedsedsteen* (Heidelberg) includes tape and tape experiments with issues, as does *Gronk* (Toronto), D. r. Wagner's *Runcible Spoon* evolved virtually into a way of life—"a communication, a place, a time/for killing floor while waiting, a person, an idea . . . a concrete poem of all of us together . . . an attempt at being human." About the magazine *Poesie Vivante* (Geneva) there gathered "P.V. Groups," an international society which "goes far beyond the magazine as such—a movement which is incontestably playing its part in the struggle for world peace and *rapprochement* between peoples." Its multilingual texts have led it toward "a new humanism integrating poetry more and more into daily life and ensuring a place for it amongst international exchanges."

The spirit of streets, poetry readings, and celebrations further expanded the role of the little magazines. One of the earliest street poets, Doug Palmer (also known as Facino) helped publish a magazine with Dave Hazelton called *Synapse* in Berkeley in 1964 which celebrated this kind of work. Palmer, who actually made a living writing poems on the streets in the Bay Area, subsequently held readings at the IWW Union hall which resulted in his publishing a huge anthology, *Poems Read in the Spirit of Peace and Gladness* (Berkeley, 1966). *Poets at Le Metro* (N.Y.C., 1964) and *Poets at the Gate* (Cleveland, 1966) were other publications based on readings and tribal gatherings. *The Anthology* (Noh Directions Press, 1968) edited by John Oliver Simon and Richard Krech, grew directly out of the first Conference of Small Magazine Editors and Publishers in Berkeley. John

Sinclair's Artists Workshop Press in Detroit, a prolific mimeo publisher in the mid-sixties, was the virtual life center for all manner of art, publishing, and living. "Free Poems," "Free Poems among Friends" (Berkeley), "Poems to People" (San Francisco), and "Free Love Periodically" (Cleveland) were some of the many irregular broadsheets and pamphlets circulated in this country out of the tribal energy of the poetry and literature of the times. Even the names would not stay still (a librarian's nightmare!): Levy's *Marrahwannah Quarterly* was also called *Marijuana Quarterly* or *Majoon Quarterly*; Marvin Malone's *Wormwood Review* has also been titled *Warm Wood, Ride You, Worm Would Rape You, The Worm Oil on View,* and so on. *Quixote* has never repeated a size or binding. *Hanging Loose* (N.Y.C.) has no binding at all; loose pages are enclosed in an envelope which serves (and is printed) as a cover.

In these ways and more the little magazine began to acquire a new definition for itself, to become an ever-changing, moving process, a string of continuous events more than a series of contained and individual issuances. Hence, John Oliver Simon could say of the frequency of *Aldebaran Review,* "published when it happens," and mean it. The *chrono-logique* of periodical publishing had been consumed by a vastly larger *psycho-logique,* at least for the publishers.

The United States is, and probably will continue to be, a relatively hostile (or at least unrewarding) environment for concrete poetry. But for the independent little magazines and presses of the sixties an entire worldwide experiment in communication would have passed us by. It must have something to do with the absurd international postures we find ourselves cast in today; I don't know. It will be long enough before courses of study in this genre will be permitted to pass through the ivy of even the hippiest universities. And then a veritable time warp must occur before its acceptance by such Americans as Rep. William Scherle of Iowa, who commented on the inclusion of Aram Saroyan's one-word experiment "LIGHGHT" in the *American Literary Anthology* thus: "Culture should not be spoon-fed to an effete elite at the

131

expense of the general public. There exists in this country a thing called free enterprise. If seven-letter words turn on some people, then they should pay for the joy rather than force our hard-working taxpayers to subsidize their cultural taste."

If concrete poetry in the United States, Canada, and England is, in part at least, bound into the mimeograph movement of the mid-sixties, that movement in its turn is bound centrally into the entire small press movement. I call 1965 the year of "peak activity" for the mimeos. As shown in table 1 only 5 percent of the little magazines in 1960 were mimeo produced. By 1965 nearly one-fourth (23 percent) were mimeos, with some decrease (to 15 percent) toward the last year of the decade. Paralleling this, from 1960 to 1965, was the movement to offset production, indicating a generally similar motivating force and spirit; and the subsequent decline in mimeos (1966 to 1969) points to a final meshing of the two forces. Such magazines as *Grande Ronde Review, Goliards,* and *Tampa Poetry Review,* once devoutly mimeographed (and all, incidentally, starting in 1964), have gone over to offset printing since mid-decade, the first two at least with radical changes in format. Others—*Poetry Newsletter, Wild Dog, Marrahwannah Quarterly, Olé,* and *Outcast*—have ceased publication.

Nor is there a technological explanation for this flourishing. Invented in 1878 by Thomas Edison, the machine has since changed almost not at all in principle, and accessory equipment (such as feeders and interlevers) is still very simple (and far from perfect). The most significant advances have been along the lines of the German Gestetner, a relative of the mimeograph, and in electronic stencil cutting and silk screening. Most small-press mimeo publishers I know, however, operate used hand-driven equipment and cut stencils on the same old mechanical typewriters used for manuscripts and letters. Perhaps the single greatest technical advantage borne by the mimeo machine is speed, a critical feature to a time where contemporaniety meant everything. And as both typesetter and printer, the editor had full control over the timing and general quality of his publication.

The mimeo movement was located primarily in four countries: England, Canada, Brazil, and the United States. Three "poeteditorpublishers" of imposing influence in the United States were d. a. Levy of Cleveland, John Sinclair of Detroit, and Douglas Blazek of Bensenville, Illinois. They were most active between 1964 and 1967; none is now publishing with any regularity: Levy is dead, Sinclair is in jail, and Blazek discontinued his imprints when he moved to California.

Now known for such excellent collections as *All Gods Must Learn to Kill* (Analecta Press, 1968, poems) and *Life in a Common Gun* (Quixote, 1968, letters between poets), Blazek became, with his Mimeo Press and *Open Skull,* the virtual energy center of a kind of tough, irreverent poetry sometimes called "meat poetry" ("the open skull is tearing w/acid fingers at its adipose . . . hooks must enter the meat trapped w/in the bone. Dignities must be set aside . . . the phosphoric substance of soul must be unleashed from phlegm and fizz and puncture the hymen of reality!" From an essay titled "A Primer on Open Skull Pressology" in *Marrahwannah Quarterly,* v.3, no.1, 1967). Dedicated to "the cause of making poetry dangerous," still an imperative in Blazek's poetry, he published, attacked, cajoled, and otherwise promoted such poets as Steven Richmond (whose own magazine, *Earth,* in Santa Monica, at one point even outraged its own contributors), Charles Bukowski (toughest and most persistenly published poet in *all* the little magazines throughout the decade), William Wantling (a sometime drug poet of enormous lyrical talent whom Walter Lowenfels has called "the best poet of his age"), Brown Miller (poet and essayist, perhaps the genre's most articulate critical voice), T. L. Kryss (one of Cleveland's most senstive poet-artists whose silk-screen covers are a distinguishing feature of many of the publications of this genre), d. a. Levy, D. r. Wagner, and many, many others. While he did verge on collage and concrete poetry in the Levy vein (e.g., *Homage to the Squares, the Blacks, Ian Hamilton, Finlay and Marshall McLuhan,* 1968), Blazek was primarily an essayist, poet, and proselytizer. Few small magazines, mimeo or otherwise, are untouched by his influence. (See *Nola Express,* New Orleans, and *Kaleidoscope,*

Milwaukee, for some of his current reviews; an article-profile on him, "Revelation of the Iceberg's Mass," by Joel Deutsch, appears in *Small Press Review,* v.2, no.1.)

Levy, of course, was in close spiritual and material alliance with Blazek and the *Olé* poets. In *Marrahwannah Quarterly* (v.2, no.4) he mentions that each issue from *Open Skull* "contains bloody fingerprints of Doug Blazek who prints almost as much as I do." Their proximity and prolixity are fact, and Levy's writing and publishing bore an ever-expanding energy into the global village. But what moved him, foremost and finally, was the American industrial city of Cleveland, Ohio, there on the shores of what the Cleveland poets called "Swamp Erie" (they even published a series of books called *The Polluted Lake Series*). "This town has been here for 150 years and has managed to murder every poet and painter who has been here," he told Andrew Curry in an interview (*Dust,* no.12). "I Wrote about Cleveland as I saw it. I was very young when I wrote *Cleveland Undercovers* [7 Flowers Press, 1966] . . . I was only nineteen or twenty . . . I'm twenty-four [now]. And that's *old* in Cleveland." He likened Cleveland (and the United States, in fact) to Nazi Germany, but he stayed. Besides *Marrahwannah Quarterly,* which published such Cleveland poets as rjs, T. L. Kryss, Kent Taylor, D. r. Wagner, Carl Woideck, and Thom Szuter, he edited several anthologies, most notably *465, An Anthology of Cleveland Poets* (7 Flowers Press, 1966), *Three-Oh-Six,* an anthology of Cleveland Poets (7 Flowers Press, 1967), and *Cleveland Concrete* (Free Love Press, 1966). Of his many books, collections, and pamphlets, *Cleveland: Rectal Eye Visions* (Niagara: Today, 1966) with an introduction by Doug Blazek, *UKANHAVYRFUCKINCITIBAK* (Asphodel Bookshop, 1967), and *Unmailed Letters to Ed Pederson and the (Mysterious) Annburgers* (Canada: Fleye Press, 1967), a collection of concrete letters, are all especially notable.

John Sinclair, the gentle, burly giant Detroit poet/editor is a revolution by himself. Moving through his community of artists there—a place to him not unlike Cleveland was to Levy—he put his mark on virtually everything produced by the Artists Workshop Press. In the huge mimeo magazine

Work, he published a continuing "Active Anthology" which was centered on local poets. "The idea is to offer a place, a forum, for work that does come out of our community situation, and in such a manner as to offer encouragement and stimulation to people many of whom are just beginning to write, read, etc. . . . Poetry is finally an oral art." His commitment to Detroit as a community, to her artists, and to poetry, music, and working people was sincere and unwavering. Yet Sinclair and his friends—like Levy and his—were subjected to police harassment almost from the beginning, ending for Sinclair in jail. His important work: magazines—*Work* (poetry), *Change* (music), *Whe're* (reviews, news), and *Guerrilla,* "a monthly newspaper of kulchur" (which incorporated *Change* and *Whe're*); books—*The Leni Poems, Meditations, A Suite for John Coltrane, The Poem for Warner Stringfellow.* A record, *Firemusic* by Sinclair, was also published by AWP.

The mimeo movement in the United States and elsewhere had a scope that reached far beyond Blazek, Levy, and Sinclair. A full history is overdue but cannot, of course, be taken up here except in very cursory outline. Out of Cleveland to California (via Niagara Falls) was D. r. Wagner (*Runcible Spoon*) who contributed greatly to the movement, and who even now uses a Gestetner and, as noted earlier, has moved toward concrete and environmental poetry (his glass poetry may be the most exquisite this side of Finlay). Among his own books are *Defining Zero Spaceforms from a Chairswing* (*Canada*: Fleye Press, 1967), *18th Century Egyptian Automobile Turnon* (Poetry Est. 1966, 1967), and *The Egyptian Stroboscope* (Asphodel Bookshop, 1966) which includes work by d. a. Levy. *Moonstones* and *The Eight Pager* were his earlier mimeo mags published from Niagara Falls. *Runcible Spoon* started in 1968, and his latest (coedited by Ingrid Swanberg) is *My Landlord Must Be Really Upset.*

From Buffalo is *Intrepid,* edited by Allen DeLoach, which carries a Lower East Side influence from the editor's early days there and verges toward antirealism and cut-up poetry. (The cover of *Intrepid* is calligraphed by Brion Gysin, a founder of the Domaine Poetique in Paris, which frequently performs his work.) The primary mimeo influence out of the Southeast was Duane Locke's massive *Poetry Review* (University of Tampa), guided by his inclination for "linguistic reality—a self-contained interior cosmos," though almost all manner of work has been published. In New York City *Kauri,* edited by Will Inman, published (and is publishing) hundreds of poems, letters, and comments in "search of self" through the literary medium; Kirby Congdon's annual *Magazine* encouraged "experiment, exposure, trial-and-error"; Diane Di Prima's *Floating Bear* was a revolutionary newsletter of poetry, and an adjunct to her well-known Poets' Press; Wally Depew's *Poetry Newsletter,* in the editor's somewhat preexperimental days, published news of the mimeo scene, reviews, essays, and poetry; and in Brooklyn, Harvey Tucker's *Black Sun* published work more along the lines of Locke's linguistic reality than Levy's concrete or Blazek's meat poetry.

The other strong mimeo influence of the mid-sixties came out of the Northwest, which in magazines like Ben Hiatt's *Grande Ronde Review,* Charles Potts' *Litmus,* and Mel Buffington's *Blitz* exuded, however briefly, a startling regional poetry that possessed both land and social-protest qualities. *Salted Feathers,* edited in Pullman, Washington, and Portland, Oregon, by Dick Bakken was far more nationally oriented; Jerry Paul Simpson's *Aspects* (Eugene, Oregon) was a "literary potpourri for left-wing socialists."

The Canadian movement turned on David Harris' Fleye Press (Toronto and Vancouver), whose multimedia interests are now closely allied with the Ganglia Press group in Toronto. This includes bp Nichol, David Aylward, Bill Bissett, and others, and has had working lines to the Cleveland poets and to D. r. Wagner and other West Coast small presses. Also in Canada was Nelson Ball's *Weed* (Kitchener, Ontario) and Len Gasparini's *Mainline* (Windsor, Ontario).

In England the mimeo movement has been greatly influenced by global concrete poetry and the search for international communication and peace. In many and often quiet ways these magazines have been more radical in approach than their American brethren. Notable are Dave Cunliffe's *Poet-meat* (now *PM Newsletter*); Tlaloc, edited by Cavan

McCarthy, a young (twenty-seven) experimenter/librarian of great personal dimension and knowledge; and *Nebulum's Olive Dachshund,* edited by Glyn Pursglove. In neighboring Belgium, *Labris* is a large multilingual mimeo "dedicated to the avant garde." The Indian magazine *Damn You/A Magazine of the Arts* (Bombay), edited by Arvind Krishna Mehrotra and Alok Rai, also belongs to the movement, as do Mehrotra's *Ezra,* a "new *imagisme"* mag, and *Fakir,* a magazine of religious and mystical poetry.

In Brazil, mimeo publishing was by far the most inchoate in the world, despite the interesting fact that it began about 1964 when a good many Americans and British were also beginning, pointing to the global nature of the *Zeitgeist.* The Brazilian movement was started by a writer, Geraldo Carvalho, and friends in João Pessoa (Paraíba), who established *Edicoes Caravela* and *Edicoes Sanhaua* in 1964. That and other mimeo publishing involved prose more than poetry, mostly short stories by such as Carvalho, Paulo Melo, and María José Limeira. Needless to say, the quality of these short stories was special, showing the existentialist influences of Beckett and Camus and the antirealism of the Argentine Jorge Luis Borges. Carvalho's "Pink Asphalt" and Virginius de Gama e Mello's "The Beings" are exemplary. Early magazines were *Saga* (Belo Horizonte), *Encuentro* (São Paulo), *Iapetos* (Macaé), and *Azulejo* (São Luís).

Then, beyond the three major influences discussed—printing technology, concrete poetry, and the spirit of mimeography—there are many other influences, most of them more confined geographically or more spiritually particular. Few magazines, for example, were untouched by the poetry of Charles Bukowski, probably the most published poet of the decade, tough as wire, Dada-like, always saying it the way it comes down to him, incessantly fascinated with the very act of making the poem and often cataloging the environment in his last several lines. He published stories as early as 1944; his first poem was printed in 1956 in *Quixote* (Cornwall-on-Hudson); by 1959 his poetry began to appear widely in little magazines such as *Epos* (Crescent City, Florida), *Coffin*

(Eureka, California), and *Wanderlust* (Metairie, Louisiana). His first collection of poetry, highly surrealistic, was *Flower, Fist and Bestial Wail* (Eureka: Hearse Press) in 1961. He was named "Outsider of the Year" by Jon and Gypsy Lou Webb's *Outsider* (New Orleans) in 1962. His first important collection was published by the Webbs in 1963 (*It Catches My Heart in Its Hands*). His stock rose considerably in 1964 and 1965 when the mimeo publishers, then just starting up, seized upon Bukowski and structured a poetry and a dialogue around him. Chief among them was Douglas Blazek of *Olé,* but Steve Richmond of *Earth* (Santa Monica), d. a. Levy of Cleveland, and Charles Potts of *Litmus* (Seattle-Berkeley) were eventually included, among others. The two important collections *about* Bukowski and his work are Hugh Fox's *Bukowski* (Abyss Publications, 1969) and Blazek's *A Bukowski Sampler* (*Quixote,* 1969).

Neither unrelated to Bukowski nor the meat poets nor mimeography nor anything else in small press publishing was that thing known as free press and speech. Though the breakthroughs made by, for example, the "beats" in the fifties are to be remembered and cited, the sixties saw its share of busts, starting perhaps with the prosecution in Marin County, California, of Henry Miller's *Tropic of Cancer* and running on through Lenore Kandel's *Love Book* in San Francisco toward the latter part of the decade. These cases had the benefit of huge publicity at least. Yet throughout the decade the small poets and publishers and booksellers were busted at a rate far greater—and with far more painful results—than their larger brethren: d. a. Levy, John Sinclair, Steve Richmond, James Lowell, John Kois, Robert Head, rjs, Dave Cunliffe, Malay Roy Choudhury—the list goes on round the world and back into the heart and soul of Western reason and constitutional guarantees. At present Allen Ginsberg is collecting such documented evidence for P.E.N.

A number of black presses sprang up by mid-decade (there are now dozens): Dudley Randall's Broadside Press (Detroit), which has published several dozen very fine one-sheet poems and some full-length books (*Black Pride* by Don L. Lee; *For Malcolm: Poems on the Life and Death of Malcolm X,* edited by Randall and Margaret Burroughs); *Soulbook* (Berkeley), one of the earliest magazines (1964), "dedicated to all our black ancestors who have made it possible for us to exist and work for a LOVE SUPREME of BLACK PEOPLE"; *Journal of Black Poetry* (San Francisco), edited by Joe Gonsalves; and *Black Dialogue* (San Francisco) edited by Arthur Sheridan, Edward Spriggs, and Abdul Karim. Because of the political and social imperatives of the black movement in this country, it must be said that the underground newspapers have served as a more immediately effective medium. Black poets and writers have insisted on coming to the small magazines more as poets and writers than as blacks. Andrew Curry (*Dust*), Al Young (*Love*), and Ed Bullins (an editor of the now defunct *Ante*) are cases in point.

As part of the attack on tradition and taxonomy, many small magazines coveted nonspecialization as a policy. Among them foremost was Harry Smith's *The Smith* (N.Y.C.), "the most general magazine," now occupied in the promulgation of Smith's "Anti-Civilization League"; Curt Johnson's *December* (Western Springs, Illinois); Morris Edelson's *Quixote* (Madison); Margaret Randall's *El Corno Emplumado* (Mexico City), a magazine of great range, quality, and influence; Marvin Malone's *Wormwood Review* (Storrs, Connecticut); and *Dust* (El Cerrito, California), which I myself founded with others of widely disparate (too widely, it turned out) interests in 1964. The "imagism" of the fifties was carried into the sixties by Robert Bly's *Sixties* (Madison, Minnesota) and George Hitchcock's *Kayak* (San Francisco), among others. A poetry written after the spirit of the American Indian appeared on the West Coast about 1966, exemplary of which are "Shaman Songs" by Gene Fowler and Norman Moser, published in Moser's *Illuminations* and in *Dust*.

Though in the times few magazines could maintain any genuine regional flavor for long, some did at least in part covet a geography or what might be called a "geo-sociology." These would include such magazines as *Foxfire* (Rabun Gap, Georgia), edited by G. Eliot Wigginton; *South and West* (Fort Smith, Arkansas), edited by Sue Abbott Boyd; John Sinclair's *Artists Workshop Press* (Detroit); d. a. Levy's *Mar-*

rahwannah Quarterly (Cleveland); John Simon's *Aldebaran Review* (Berkeley); and R. R. Cuscaden's *Midwest* (Geneva, Illinois). Also, as mentioned previously, the northwestern mimeo publishing of Ben Hiatt's *Grande Ronde Review,* Mel Buffington's *Blitz,* and Carlos Reye's *Prensa de Lagar* exuded a regional quality.

Shortly after mid-decade, government money began to appear for the small magazines from both the National Endowment for the Humanities and the Coordinating Council of Literary Magazines, a New York-based nonprofit association; and George Plimpton and Peter Ardery brought out their first *American Literary Anthology* in 1966, designed to print the best work each year from the small magazines. As might be expected, of course, the small and truly independent magazines were the last to benefit from these programs, and a number of things have conspired to make even dimmer the hope of future beneficence. Largest is the insistence on congressional and other administrative meddling ("auditing") in the programs and, as Representative Scherle's remarks cited earlier here, a gross intolerance for letting art go its way. All this has led to the virtual shut-off of funds in the Plimpton project and to a Washington-based audit of the Coordinating Council. There is also in the National Endowment itself a new leadership, oriented more toward community programs, and away from support of individual artists or independent (let alone clandestine) efforts. Finally, there is, in the face of any and all institutional interference, beneficient or otherwise, the irascibility and impatience of the small pressman himself, who cherishes his freedom more than his very life. Those well-meaning administrators caught between these impulses and a government which cherishes the opposite have a thankless, bitter, and probably failing task.

And then the small presses organized themselves in 1968 at Berkeley into the Committee of Small Magazine Editors and Publishers (COSMEP), a difficult undertaking given the above-mentioned editorial attitudes. Yet COSMEP has somehow stayed glued together despite periodic financial emergencies, has in three years held three annual conferences (Berkeley, 1968; Ann Arbor, 1969; Buffalo, 1970), and has published a *Catalogue of Small Press Publications* in 1969 (free to libraries) and a *Bookstore Survey* (1969) for members. It also issues a periodical newsletter ($5 a year to nonmembers).

This getting together—however tenuous at present—has been one marker at least that the sixties are gone and that a new era is upon us. I believe that government support in the future will run from spotty to nil, and actually be less and less significant to the small presses. *At the same time* I look for continued consolidation along economic lines as editors rework and harden the increasing power of their numbers. I suppose this process is bound to affect them editorially, though if they stand clear of institutional sanction, these effects are not likely to be serious. What *is* likely, however, is that small pressmen will find themselves with growing power as a pressure group, and what lies beyond *that* is anybody's guess. Certainly individual presses and editors will be less and less at the mercy of commercial printers, the post office, cheating bookstores, and county prosecutors. In addition to COSMEP's 250-member publishers there is the Underground Press Syndicate of newspapers which, with its associate, Canadian, and European presses, has nearly two hundred members; the Association of Little Presses in the United Kingdom has about sixty members; and the COPLAI group in Argentina (Confederación de Publicaciones Literarias Independentes) has an unknown number. Too, there are many more "specialized" magazines and presses dealing with the interests of blacks, Indians, women, Mexican Americans, and gays, and with issues of ecology, educational reconstitution, G.I. antiwar movements (seventy-five of the last in the United States alone).

Put it all together by, say, 1975, and you will indeed have a new age.

Bibliography

The assignment here was "to supplement Hoffman." "Hoffman" refers to the late Frederick J. Hoffman of the University of Wisconsin, one of the authors (with Charles

141

Allen and Carolyn F. Ulrich) of *The Little Magazine: A History and Bibliography* (Princeton, 1946), of which copies are available (unless you can find an old original) through University Microfilms, Ann Arbor, Michigan, for about $18. In this massive work was included a main bibliography of more than five hundred items, with a supplementary bibliography of about one hundred items, all arranged chronologically from 1891 to 1945. Each item contains up to eleven "details," from title and "publishing body" to index information and key symbols for the libraries where the magazines were studied. In my own bibliography I have been able to delineate the following details: (1) title and subtitle; (2) publishing body, if any (the nature of the sixties, and so of the little magazine, and so of this listing, reduces the number of such support bodies to insignificance); (3) the place of publication, with changes noted and dates given where important; (4) the original date and the closing date, years only in most cases, with a "plus" indicating currency (as in Hoffman) and a question mark indicating unknown data; (5) frequency; and (6) editors, also with changes and dates. Irregularities, suspensions, supplements, special issues, index, and reprint information are, where available and germane, incorporated into the descriptive text (Hoffman took separate and more special account of these).

There are over one hundred items in this bibliography, chosen for their contributions to the spirit of small press publishing in the sixties and as exemplary of the "new" literature. An effort has also been made to establish in the list an international flavor—since that was a major force in the sixties—with the inclusion of items from England, France, Germany, India, and South America. Very few items are listed that took up publication after 1967, for I believe that during 1968 (the year that, for instance, the Committee of Small Magazine Editors and Publishers was established) a new era in small press publishing was upon us. And including the years 1968, 1969, and 1970, would thrust upon me the compilation of a bibliography at least triple the size of the present one. Even for those peak five years, 1963–67, the list here is quite selective.

The important difference between my list and Hoffman's is then, quite obviously, that his was an exhaustive historical effort done with at least some academic detachment; mine is the running chronicle of a committed small pressman, bound neck and foot to the immediacy and reality of his material; mine is meant only as an indicator of what was there in the decade, and an indicator only of the independent and volatile little magazine; his definitions were perhaps firmer in 1946—his supplement is meant to include those "that do not answer strictly to the definition of a little magazine"; such rigorous definition was, given the nature of the sixties, of little practical value in this present work.

As concerns sources, my own library is at least as extensive as any other private library of its kind for the decade of the sixties, and especially is it extensive in the face of a listing as biased at this one. In all cases at least *some* of the issues of each magazine were studied; in many cases, of course, all the issues were on hand. Furthermore, *study* is used here advisedly, for while in preparing this present compilation I reviewed my material carefully, that material, and more often than not the human beings who produced it, was throughout the decade a living part of my daily existence, as it is today. I wrote reviews of many of these items straight upon publication; and all of them have been incorporated issue by issue into my extensive files of small press information.

The *Directory of Little Magazines and Small Presses,* 1964 to 1970, was used as a primary guide for selecting. Supplemental data were taken from the massive files of *The Small Press Review* (Dustbooks, 1966–70), those of *The Small Press Record of Books* (Dustbooks, 1969), and those of the *Directory of Small Press/Magazine Editors and Publishers* (Dustbooks, 1970). Further references were made to *The International Guide* (*Trace,* 1960), *The Catalogue of Small Press Publications* (COSMEP 1969), the *Underground Digest* (Underground Communications, Inc., 1967), the *Underground Press Guide* (The Other Press Publishing Co., 1967), the *Second Directory of Periodicals* (Alan Swallow, 1965), and *The Catalogue of Little Press Books in Print Published in the United Kingdom* (ALP, 1970). Absolutely invaluable

143

were issues of *Trace* through the sixties, which published an "Evolving Directory." I wish, incidentally, to express here my sincere gratitude to James Boyer May, *Trace's* tough editor, for making his private data, current and past, available to me.

Abyss. Dunkirk, New York (1966–68); Somerville, Massachusetts (1969–70). 1966+ irregular. Editor: Gerard Dombrowski.

The scope of this magazine broadens from "literature in any form considered" (1967–68), to "life in any form considered" (1969–70) as Dombrowski engages also in book publishing, most notably *Bukowski* by Hugh Fox (1969), *Countdown on an Empty Streetcar* by Hugh Fox (1969), *Towards the 1970's* by Dick Higgins (1968), and *Computers for the Arts* by Dick Higgins (1969). *Abyss* has published "The Existentialism of Albert Moravia," a continuing article by Joan Ross and Donald Freed, fiction by Henry H. Roth and Herbert Feldman, and poetry by E. R. DuFrense, Gerald Locklin, R. H. Atkinson. Editor has an abiding obsession in private life with Zen Philosophy, especially that of Alan Watts.

The Activist. Oberlin, Ohio. 1960+ triannual. Editors: Dennis Hale (up to 1966. In 1965 with Mitch Cohen and W. C. McWilliams; in 1966 with Glenn Eric Roberts); Glenn Eric Roberts (1967–68); Stormy Tatter, Michael Charney (1969–70).

Earlier issues carry poetry, fiction, criticism, with articles on politics, economics, and social relations. In the latter part of the sixties, space is largely given to student politics, cartoons, letters, essays, and reviews. "We are an independent student political magazine attempting to provide a forum for discussion and critical analysis. Although radical, we seek discussion and insight; not polemics and dogma" (1968).

Agora, Jornal Literario. Divinopolis (M.G.), Brazil. 1967+ monthly. Editor: Lazaro Barreto.

Agora is a large (13 by 18 inch) newsprint tabloid in Portuguese which publishes poetry, fiction, art, criticism. Often translates from other languages, and seeks contact with young people interested in modern life and culture. Has published works by Osvaldo André de Melo, Ricardo Marques, Katia Bento, and Marcio Almeida.

Alcor. Asunción, Paraguay. 1960+ bimonthly. Editor: Ruben Barerio Saguier.

Publishes the new poetry, fiction, news, and interviews. Interested in all things on culture and literature that reflect the Guarani avant garde. (e.g., "analogias entre el guayaki y el guarani paraguayo," no.32, Sept.-Oct. 1964). Work has appeared by Evelio Fernandez Arevalo, Gustavo Gonzalez, Roque Vallejos and Hugo Rodriquez Alcala.

Aldebaran Review. Berkeley, California. 1968+ published "when the changes are right." Editors: John Oliver Simon, Alta.

AR is one of the Noh Directions Press outputs (with *Avalanche*), John Oliver Simon and Richard Krech, publishers. It is important as a direct politico-poetic outgrowth of late-sixties Berkeley politics which culminated in the spring 1969 "People's Park" demonstrations. *AR* number 3 claims to be published by a "small hired gang of yellow running dog editors and is dedicated to the final revolution." "Any real poem," says Simon, "whatever its subject is a weapon in the hands of your brothers. Any false poem is a tool in the fingers of the great business conspiracy . . . it's not easy to handle the messages. Almost every poet I take seriously is strung out in an impossible mental position trying to keep up . . . watch out for verbs that move both ways at once." *AR* number 7 is a special collection of poems by Charles Potts, known then in Berkeley as "Laffing Water." In eight issues *AR* published poems by Doug Palmer, Mary Norbert Korte, Gail Dusenberry, Pete Winslow, Douglas Blazek, Patricia Parker, Brown Miller, and many others. John Thomson (of Berkeley's "Filthy Speech Movement") is a regular contributor, and in *AR* number 8, his "Short History of Western Civilizations" opens the issue: the gun/the Bible/whiskey. By his last issue, Spring 1970, Simon had moved somewhat away from radical street politics toward ecology and the green revolution.

American Haiku. Platteville, Wisconsin (in cooperation with School of Arts and Sciences, Wisconsin State University). 1963–69‖ semiannual. Editors: James E. Bull, Gayle Bull; poetry editors: Robert Spiess, Gary Brower (until 1968).

Alleged to be the first magazine devoted exclusively to the development of English-language haiku. Even though somewhat limited to publishing original haiku by subscribers only, the scope of its material is broader, and its presentation cleaner, than most of its contemporary brethren (*Haiku, Kaiku Highlights, Haiku West, Sonnet CinQuain Tanka Haiku, The Blue Print*). Runs consistently thoughtful reviews of contemporary haiku books and maintains a periodical record of such books. Publishes articles such as "The Study of the Season Reference in American Haiku" by James Bull, and "Japanese Life in Contemporary Senryu" by Akira Kimura. Engages in book publishing (*County Seat* by Clement Hoyt, *The Heron's Legs* by Robert Spiess, *Marsh-Grasses* by O. Southard).

American Weave. Cleveland, Ohio, 1963–69 (?), semiannual. Editors: Alfred Cahen, David French.

James L. Weil is advisory editor. The late Loring Williams was founder and editor emeritus. In 1965, Williams turned the magazine over to Cahen and French and moved to Maine to establish the *American Weave Press,* which brought out several hardcover books of poetry (*Houses of Ice* by Alfred B. Cahen, *Four Corridors* by David C. French, *Brother Crow* by Williams). As a magazine, *AW* published Hart Crane memorabilia and reviews by Lewis Turco, Joseph Joel Keith, Ulmont Ives, and others. *AW* has "one primary editorial objective: To publish the finest possible quality of poetry and other material . . . without influence of schools or trends, public or private complaints, or extenal pressures."

Ann Arbor Review. Ann Arbor, Michigan. 1967+ quarterly. Editor: Fred Wolven.

Has published poetry by Duane Locke, Harvey Tucker, Sam Cornish, Hugh Fox, and many others; fiction by David Madden, Elisavietta Ritchie, and Russell Banks. *AAR* also publishes reviews of small-press books.

Ante. Los Angeles, California, 1964–68|| quarterly. Editors: William Harris (1965); Norma Alquist, Frances Colvin, Isabelle Ziegler, Vera Hickman (1967–68).

Ante was in the van of the small-press movement of the sixties, starting in that critical year along with multitudes of other magazines and underground newspapers (e.g., the *Los Angeles Free Press*). In early issues, Ed Bullins edited the poetry; Harry Deutsch the fiction; and Isabelle Ziegler, Sam Eisenstein, and Vera Hickman served as associates. From the beginning *Ante* featured a large quantity of good, new stories by such writers as James D. Houston, Josephine Carson, Jack Matthews, Ed Bullins, Albert Drake, and Deena Metzger.

Approach, A Literary Quarterly. Rosemont, Pennsylvania. Spring 1947–Summer 1967, quarterly. Editors: Helen Morgan Brooks, Albert Fowler, Helen Fowler, et al.

Always somewhat traditional, these editors still managed to publish some poets found in more radical environs—Charles Bukowski, Robert Lax, John Oliver Simon, as well as work by James Laughlin, Thomas Merton, and Kenneth Rexroth. "*Approach* early decided to exist on the periphery and forego the prerequisites and obscenities conferred by the company of arm twisters, back scratchers and face slappers. Even so, the managing editors have been threatened with violence and judges of poetry prizes with subornation." Important because it spans two eras, the postwar beat and the sixties activism. Number 64 is a cumulative index to all past issues.

Approches, "Revue de Recherches." Paris. 1966+ quarterly. Editors: Jean François Bory, Julien Blaine.

True to its title from the first, *Approches* under J. F. Bory and J. Blaine has been an exemplary force in the European approach to the word as graphic raw material, an approach which also includes Ugo Carrega's *Tool* (Milan), Pierre Garnier and Martino Oberto's *Ana Eccetera* (Paris and Genoa) and, in the United States, Wally Depew's *PN2 Experiment* (Sacramento, California) and Dick Higgins' Something Else Press (N.Y.C.). The work is variously called "concrete," "word-plastics," etc., and is important throughout the decade in its loosening effect on traditional boundaries between the

147

genres of art. *Approches* has published work by Bory, Blaine, Augusto de Campos, Haroldo de Campos, Kitasono Katue, Ernest Jandl, Claude Pelieu, and many others. Special issues include *Bêche* and *Whispering,* both by J. F. Bory.

Artists Workshop Press. Detroit and Ann Arbor, Michigan. c. 1964–(?). Editor: John Sinclair (and others including Ron Caplan, Robin Eichele, Charles Moore, Gary Grimshaw, Dave Sinclair).

Few poet-editors have had as much going at one time as John Sinclair, who on top of it all has been subjected to continuous police harassment, harassment which at this writing has ended in jail for him. At one time or another in the mid-sixties he edited three huge mimeo publications: *Work,* a magazine of fiction, poetry, articles, and art; *Whe're,* a magazine of reviews of contemporary poetry and prose; *Change,* a magazine of contemporary jazz criticism, reviews of records, photos, poems, and essays about contemporary music. He was also head of something in Ann Arbor called "Trans-Love Energies," under which loosely were found Trans-Love Productions, *Warren-Forrest Sun* (a newspaper), MC5 Enterprises, Trans-Love Light 7 Poster Co., UP Enterprises, Detroit Lamar, The Store. He was also connected with the Detroit underground newspaper *Guerrilla,* edited by Alan Van Newkirk. In addition to this, he brought out many good titles under the Artists' Workshop Press imprint, including Diane Di Prima's *Revolutionary Letters, Friends Living and Dead* by David Federman, and Sinclair's *Meditations, A Suite for John Coltrane.*

Aspects. Eugene, Oregon. 1964+ irregular. Editor: Jerry Paul Simpson; occasional assistant and associate editors: Leo David Feldman, Michael Brophy, Mike Mikkelson, Richard Reed.

This magazine is important as a fiercely independent participant in the "mimeo revolution" of the mid-sixties. It is a "literary potpourri for left-wing extremists" (1966) and a magazine of "social protest and fiction" (1967). The magazine is constantly outstanding for its commentary (e.g., a "six-issue indictment of America") *and* for its discovery of short, contemporary fiction by T. D. C. Kuch, W. C. Bondarenko, Peggy Taub, Curt Johnson, and others. Occasional reprints of social import appear, such as Carl Ogleby's "Statement to the Thirty-Five Thousand" in the August 1967 issue, and Henry Anderson's "A Case against the Drug Culture" (April 1968). It grew to be one of the best illustrated of the mimeos (e.g., in the January 1969 issue with Dick Lord). Unlike many mimeos of the mid-sixties movement, it has not changed to slick format or lithography.

Beloit Poetry Journal. Beloit, Wisconsin. 1950+ quarterly. Editors: Robert H. Glauber, David M. Stocking, Marion Kingston Stocking, John Bennett; art: Vernon Shaffer, Arthur Adair.

This magazine is important, like *Approach,* for spanning essentially two socio-literary eras, that of the beats and that of the sixties. It is additionally important for maintaining a policy of printing poetry only. "It is the function of a little poetry magazine to print good poetry and to discover new poets." Many important poets have appeared here over the years: L. C. Phillips, Peter Wild, Felix Pollak, Joyce Carol Oates, Ottone Riccio, Gil Orlovitz, Nancy Willard, R. R. Cuscaden, and so on. Several "special" issues were published in the sixties, including contemporary Philippine poetry (Summer 1964), *Tern's Bone* and other poems by Suzanne Gross (Spring 1965), *Eleven Contemporary Japanese Poets* (Spring 1966), *Concrete Poetry* (Fall 1966), *Discoveries* (New poets, Summer 1968), and *Poetry from the Chicago Ghetto Writing Workshops* (Winter 1968–69).

Black and Red. Kalamazoo, Michigan (1968–69); Detroit (1970). 1968+ irregular.

Without editors or bylines, this magazine (the press also publishes books) exists in an unusual photo-text collage motif. It "is not a new current of radical thought within capitalist society. It is a subversive action. It is a new front in the world anticapitalist struggle. It is an organic link between the theory-action of the world revolutionary movement and the action-theory of the new front." *B&R* is dedicated "to create at long last a situation which goes beyond the point of no return."

Articles such as "Exposure of the Capitalist University," and the "Revolutionary Movement in Germany" have appeared. *B&R* is spiritually allied with Madison's *Radical America* and the Situationist International group.

Black Dialogue. San Francisco. 1965–66|| irregular. Editors: Arthur Sheridan, Edward Spriggs (N.Y.), Abdul Karim.

Black Dialogue "is a meeting place for voices of the black community wherever that community may exist." *BD* published articles by LeRoi Jones ("Black Arts") and Joe Gonsalves ("The Fantasy and Its Enforcers"); illustrations by Earl Miller and Glen Miles. In volume 2 number 1 (July-August 1965) appears Ed Bullin's play "How Do You Do—A Nonsense Drama."

Black Sun. Brooklyn, New York. 1964–69|| irregular. Editor: Harvey Tucker.

Black Sun is a large (8½ by 14, averaging fifty pages) mimeo magazine belonging at the center of the mid-sixties mimeo movement, somewhat less vociferous than the meat poetry magazines, closer in style and content to Duane Locke's *Tampa Poetry Review.* "Enough said about life . . . we are here to write poems. Something deeper than personal . . . sometimes the poet's eyes pick visions that must be explained immediately. And so we give birth to a new magazine with the hope that we can fill the gap between the moment of seeing and the moment of saying! Nothing is foolish if it bothers, nothing is unreal if it IS!" *Black Sun* has published poetry by Duane Locke, Sam Cornish, and many, many others.

Blitz. LaGrande, Oregon. 1964–67|| irregular. Editors: Mel Buffington, with Bobby Watson (1965), with Jan Kepley (1966), Jan Kepley (1967); moved to Seattle in 1967 with Kepley.

This magazine is an important ingredient in the general mid-sixties mimeo movement and in the grassroots thrust out of the Northwest in 1964–65, which included Ben Hiatt's *Grande Ronde Review.* Carlos Reye's *Prensa de Lagar* and *Pliego,* Charles Potts' *Litmus.* Published by Buffington's Mad Virgin Press ("Is the virgin mad because she is a virgin or a virgin because she is mad?"), *Blitz* is exemplary of a kind of social poetry founded in the deep, red earth of the northwestern United States—work by Kepley, Reyes, Buffington, Hiatt, Watson and Ron Bayes. Additionally, *Blitz* printed work by Charles Bukowski, Philip Whalen, G. R. Morgan, Allen Ginsberg, Douglas Blazek, and Steven Richmond.

Bo Heem E Um. Greenock, Scotland. 1967 + quarterly. Editor: Thomas A. Clark.

Primarily a press with a bias toward "concrete" poetry; latest word is that *"Bo* has fallen into the South Street Publication trap. Will the editor be able to pull it out? See next issue" (1969). *Bo Heem E Um* number 3 is a collection of poetry by Charles Verey; number 5 is a collection by Thomas Clark.

Bollettino Tool. Milan, Italy. 1968 + quarterly. Editor: Ugo Carrega.

Carrega's work is integral to the essentially European movement toward plastic expression, the word as raw material (see also *Approches*), toward "the world of verbal-phonetic signs (of the words apart from their meaning or sound) and the world of graphic signs (their physical appearance, the 'matter' of the word on the page)." *Tool* number 6 contains work by Luigi Ferro, Maurizio Spatola, and others.

Boss. New York City. 1966 + semiannual. Editor: Reginald Gay.

This is a well-produced magazine interested in a great range of materials from poetry to photos. The Spring 1967 issue contains an interview by Saul Gottlieb with Jean-Jacques Lebel, poetry by Tuli Kupferberg, Julian Beck, selections from Kirby Congdon's *Dream Work,* and a one-act by Joseph Renard.

Breakthru, An International Poetry Magazine. Sussex, England. 1961–67 (?) bimonthly. Editors: Ken Geering, Alec Cornwall.

This is an unaligned magazine ("left, peace, human rights, up with Brecht, down with Beckett") of poetry, reviews, art, satire, criticism. Famous attack on Samuel Beckett ("the cult of the obscure") in 1965 won praise and damnation. Producers of many booklets including "Poetry from People," "Poetry from Left," "Poetry for Peace," and "Love Poetry."

Broadside Press. Detroit, Michigan. 1965+ monthly. Editor: Dudley Randall.

This is one of the most important black presses in the country. It has produced several dozen single-sheet broadsides of poetry, excellently printed and presented. This press has also published several softbound books, most notably *Black Arts: An Anthology of Black Creations* edited by Ahmed Alhamisi; *Black Pride* by Don L. Lee; and *For Malcolm: Poems on the Life and Death of Malcolm X,* edited by Dudley Randall and Margaret Burroughs.

Buddhist Thirdclass JunkMail Oracle. Cleveland, Ohio. 1967+ irregular. Editor: Steve Ferguson.

The late d. a. Levy apparently helped found this publication, which is of immense importance in understanding the Cleveland political-poetry scene in the latter sixties. In newsprint format, it is a panorama of cut-up, concrete and collage art, current events, poetry, articles, reviews, cartoons, photos, etc. It represents an ongoing visual and sensory effort "to communicate in this universe."

Camels Coming. Reno, Nevada (1965–68); San Francisco (1970). 1965–68; 1970+ irregular. Editor: Richard Morris. Also: Camels Hump Newsletter and CC Press.

The original full title of this mag is "I think I hear Camels Coming," a statement made, the editor tells me, by a radio announcer friend who blurted out the sentence to fill some embarrassing dead air time. The editor is a Ph.D. physicist who started *CC* at Reno, and who now is the executive secretary of the Committee of Small Magazine Editors and Publishers (COSMEP). The magazine started in 1965 lithographed and went to mimeography with issue number 7. "Camels Hump Newsletter" was changed to a Quark series of 10- to 12-page booklets in 1967. Contributors over the years included Clayton Eshelman, D. r. Wagner, Will Inman, Grace Butcher, Theodore Englin, Sharon Asselin, and many others. Notable in number 7 is an essay-review by Morris ("A New Manifesto") of the combined efforts of Charles Bukowski, Douglas Blazek, D. r. Wagner, d. a. Levy, and Brown Miller.

Casa de las Américas. Habana, Cuba. Dates unknown. Editor: Roberto Fernandez Retamar.

Published by the Organización Continental Latinoamérica de Estudiantes (*Revista Oclae*), this magazine contains contemporary work by Cubans. Special issues such as one on heroic fighters (*Guerrillero heroica*) are notable.

Caterpillar. New York City. 1967+ quarterly. Editor: Clayton Eshleman.

"A magazine in the tradition of the *Black Mountain Review* and *Transition.*"

Cineaste. New York City. 1967+ quarterly. Editor: Gary Crowdus.

This is a magazine for the young, independent filmmaker, "a magazine of cinema engagé interested in film criticism with a political consciousness; not irresponsible and raving radicalism, but sophisticated and intelligent discussion of sociopolitical impact and uses of film medium." The magazine carries reviews of films, technical advice, and criticism of the critics. An article on Pauline Kael by Richard Ayers appears in number 2 (1967); one on Andy Warhol by Andrew M. Lugg appears in number 3 (1968); an article on black filmmakers by Charles D. Peavy appears in number 8 (1969); and one on cinema and politics by Philippe Esnault is in the Winter 1969–70 issue. In the Spring 1970 issue, there is an interview with Yves de Laurot, who says *"Cinema engagé's* purpose is to create a cinema autonomous as an art and powerful as a social force."

Consumption. Seattle, Washington. 1967–(?) quarterly. Editors: Paul Hunter, Tom Parson, Patti Parson, John Sherman.

This was an important voice of the Northwest throughout the middle to late sixties. "We're small but will look hard and speak plain about anything that passes through Art's Vitals. No dogs or dogmas . . ." (1969). *Consumption* has consistently interesting art by Roger Parker, William Ward, and Kaffe Fassett; "an editorial displacement in three acts— S. A. M. Needs You" (Spring 1969); poetry by Tom Wayman, Alberta Turner, John Stevens Wade, and many others; a novel by William Rudolph. The press has also published

Tom Parson's *The Politics of Happiness or It Could Only Happen* (1968). Index to volumes 1 and 2 in volume 1, number 4 (Summer 1969).

Cormoran Y Delfin. Buenos Aires. 1964+. Editor: Ariel Canzani D.

This well-produced magazine has over the years featured poets from dozens of countries—Cuba, Portugal, Israel, every country in South America, Bulgaria, England, France—and Kirby Congdon, Tuli Kupferberg (no.16, Sept. 1968), and others from the United States. Number 19 features a "Credo Planetario" and lists many other South American magazines.

El Corno Emplumado. Mexico City. 1962+ quarterly. Editors: Sergio Mondragon and Margaret Randall (1962–68), Margaret Randall and Robert Cohen (1969+).

This magazine is one of the largest socio-literary powers in the Western Hemisphere. Originally supported by the government of Mexico, *El Corno* has been forced toward economic chaos because of Randall's sympathy with Cuba and the subsequent withdrawal of federal support. Because of her heavy political spirit, Randall has made some enemies, but over the years few, if any, editors have published as many and various poets, new and seasoned. Format is bilingual (English-Spanish). More than thirty issues have been published, some two hundred pages per issue, containing poetry, fiction, cartoons, essays, and photos. Number 31 contains a quote from the *Ho Chi Minh Prison Diary*: "People who come out of prison can build up the country. Misfortune is a test of the people's fidelity. Those who protest at injustice are people of true merit. When the prison doors are opened, the real dragon will fly out."

Cyclo-Flame (Cyclotron 1963–1966). San Angelo, Texas. 1966+ quarterly. Editor: Vernon Payne.

Payne started *Cyclotron* as a support magazine for Lilith Lorraine's *Flame Annual,* an anthology of several hundred pages. Miss Lorraine was the founder and director of Avalon, "an organization dedicated to the finding and training of new writers, who while not discarding the enduring values, courageously interpret them in the language of a changing world." In May 1966, *Flame* merged with *Cyclotron,* and was issued under the name *Cyclo-Flame*. The magazine carries work almost exclusively of Avalon members with several dozen poets published per issue.

Da-a/u dela. Milan, Italy. 1963+(?) irregular. Editors: Daniela Palazzoli, Gianni-Emilio Simonetti.

This publication belongs to the European concrete movement which includes J. F. Bory (*Approches*), Pierre Garnier (*Ana Eccetera*), Ugo Carrega (*Tool*), Wolf Vostell (*De-Collage*), Cavan McCarthy (*Tlaloc*), and others. The October 1966 issue, for instance, carries work by some twenty European concretists.

Damn You a magazine of the arts. Bombay, India. 1965+ (?) irregular. Editors: Arvind Krishna Mehrotra, Alok Rai.

This magazine, from India in English, is a genuine part of the mid-sixties mimeo movement. It bills itself as "India's first small press little mag." The editors are at odds with the "hungry generation" of Malay Roy Choudhury (who was busted for his "Stark Electric Jesus") and the Zebra avant-gardists of Calcutta. "We are illiterates, unaware of the ists/ isms. If we find a liberated soul on a creative adventure we might join him. We might let him go his way. We are not pamphleteers/ journalists/ hackwriters. Not even poets/ painters/ seers. We are men, breathing. Still, somewhere between an angel and a he-man lives a magazine of the arts" (from no.6). *DY* has published poetry by Harish Trivedi, Amit Rai, Arun Kolatkar, and others; drama by Alok Rai; work by Americans George Kimball, Douglas Blazek, and Howard McCord. In number 8 the editors down hard on the commercial avant gardists, say: "The guru-god of the Lower East Side is a very poor god because he does not even have the dignity of silence. The little gods of the rich gangetic attics of Patna and the coffee houses of Calcutta are poorer still. Avant-garde phonies are the worst." The editor is also publisher of *Ezra* (new *imagisme*) and *Fakir* (religious verse).

December, A Magazine of the Arts and Opinion. Western Springs, Illinois. 1958+ annual. Editors: Curt Johnson, Bob Wilson (movies).

This is a magazine of great range and resilience, jammed annually with over two hundred pages of poetry, fiction, articles, reviews, interviews, and commentary. The editor has himself two abiding interests: attacking the establishment tooth and nail, and discovering new short fiction (he has edited several anthologies). Latest issue features "An interview with Ernest Hemingway in Hell" by Matthew Hochberg, "Reflections on Reflections" by Maxwell Geismar, and "Radical Intellectuals and the Movement" by Paul Buhle. Each issue averages over fifty contributors in one genre or another and always features extensive movie reviews with photos. It is important for its consistently high general quality as an independent little mag art form, for its kaleidoscopic range across the arts, for its strong use of new fiction, for its longevity over the entire decade, and for its plain heft. (Reprints available through Kraus Reprint Corp.)

De-Collage. Frankfurt, Germany. Dates unknown. Editor: Wolf Vostell.

A part of the European concrete movement (see *Approches, Bollettino Tool, Tlaloc, Da-a/u dela,* etc.). Documents happenings.

Definition. New York City. 1961+ irregular. Editors: Martha Baird, Sheldon Kranz, Eli Siegel.

The press produces broadsheets and pamphlets, largely devoted to the poetry of Eli Siegel, and to his tenets of "Aesthetic Realism."

Destruction/Creation. London. 1965+. Editor: Gustav Metzger.

"A press established to further the ideas of autodestructive and autocreative art."

Diagonal Cero. Buenos Aires. 1962+ quarterly. Editor: Edgardo Antonio Vigo.

Exquisitely imaginative in production, this "open review of the contemporaneous culture" has moved significantly onto the international concrete/collage scene. Each issue is in folio form, contains "axiolography, poetry, short fiction, photos and absurdities. The editor is fighting for a real cultural approach among the artists and writers of Ibero-American culture." Concrete work by Anna Lisa Alloatti, Franz Mon, Luigi Ferro, and Haroldo de Campos has appeared.

156

Drakabygget. Orkelljunga, Sweden. Dates unknown. Editor: Jorgen Nash.

"A magazine for art, against atomic bombs, popes, and politicians. Edited by Bauhaus Situationists." Publishes poetry, articles, art, satire, and criticism.

Dust. El Cerrito, California (1964–69); Paradise, California (1969+). 1964+ quarterly. Editors: Len Fulton, Andrew Curry, and others (1964–66); Andrew Curry (1966–70); W. M. Depew (1970).

Currently coming to life again as a quarterly under the new editorship of Wally Depew after several years of irregular publication, *Dust* took itself up in that critical year of 1964 when the sixties vintage of little magazine (and the underground paper) was starting. Early issues were spotty: good fiction, bland poetry, important interviews in depth with Alan Watts, Louis Simpson, John Williams, Stephen Smale, Gene Fowler, and Doug Palmer. Issue number 12 carries an interview with the late d. a. Levy of Cleveland. Quality of poetry was strengthened under Curry, began to tend toward "guerrilla" and black poetry. Under Depew, however, and his artist-wife Linda Bandt, the magazine will carry more graphics and photos, and its thrust will inevitably be toward the international concrete scene.

Earth. Santa Monica, California. 1965–66‖ irregular. Editor: Steven Richmond.

"Creation of hate on the page, no subtlety (that to be saved for life) in creation—straight poop of pus-filled crying innards—murder on the page, breeding peace in the streets." This is how Richmond characterized his magazine, the extreme hard voice of the extreme "meat" poets of the mid-sixties, who included Charles Bukowski, Douglas Blazek of *Olé*, Brown Miller, and those who were dedicated to the "cause of making poetry dangerous." Richmond, whose vision of poetry was, in Bukowski's words, to bring it "through the fire of the bombarded graveyard," used such poetry in *Earth* that even his own contributors screeched. "No defense!" he shouted, "just don't burn it!" Richmond's book, *Hitler Painted Roses* (1966), was described by Blazek as "slimy vittles, mucus, and lily . . . sinister and scatological; not to mention their nonhumorous bath

157

in plasma, entrails, afterbirth," *Earth* flamed and burned in two hot years, and took most of the meat movement with it.

Earthquake. San Francisco, California. 1967+. Editor: Jan Jacob Herman.

This is a well-produced magazine of experimental literature, collage, cut-ups, etc. It also publishes the VDRSVP broadsheet monthly. Publishes work by Allen Ginsberg, William S. Burroughs, Claude Pelieu. Leans heavily toward experimental-concrete work; has used work by J. F. Bory and Carl Weissner, Volume 1, number 4, contains Ed Sanders' controversial piece, "The Hairy Table."

Eco Contemporaneo. Buenos Aires. 1961+ quarterly. Editor: Miguel Grinberg.

This is a small and very important "alternate press" magazine whose thrust is to "open perspectives to the consolidation of a creative attitude to surmount the actual society, and settle the basis of the future one." The editor was instrumental in the organization of COPLAI (Confederación de Publicaciones Literarias Argentinas Independentes), a group of independent magazines somewhat similar to COSMEP (Committee of Small Magazine Editors and Publishers) in the United States. Very political, *Eco Contemporaneo* celebrates Daniel Cohn-Bendit, "poder joven" (youth power), and "vida total." It is largely articles, letters, manifestos; all Spanish language.

Edge. Edmonton (Alberta), and Montreal (Quebec), Canada. 1964–68|| triannual. Editor: Henry Beissel.

For four years and nine issues ("*Edge* is honed for creativity, satire and social concern") this magazine sliced away, often flamboyantly, always intellectually and socially conscious, at Canadian establishmentarian mediocrity. Starting out as "a pedestrian offset reproduction," *Edge* by issue number 3 had gone into a professional letterpress production of over one hundred pages, "from a low-cost adventure to a more expensive commitment." *Edge* published articles, fiction, drama, satire, poetry, reviews, and art. Always interesting were Beissel's editorials, which took Canadians to task for letting U.S. business take over 60 percent of their industry (no.3), suggested throwing overboard "some of the pragmatic nonsense

introduced by Deweyitism" in education (no.4), and celebrated "the supreme power of humanization" of poetry (no.7).
In *Edge* (no.8) Beissel's editorial took the form of a long
poem titled "Czechoslovakia—Protest and Tribute."

Encuentro. Buenos Aires. 1966+ bimonthly. Editor: Al-
berto Luis Ponzo.

Starting in August of 1966 as a very thin card folio, *Encuentro* (meeting) became a slick two-color magazine by
number 7 in May 1968. Issues always include art reproduction by an Hispanic-American artist. Within its nine issues,
it has published poetry by Dionisio Aymara, Guillermo B.
Harispe, and Susan Thenon. An editorial appears in each
issue. Later numbers show a broadening interest in all Latin
American poetry.

Epos. The Work of American and British Poets. Crescent
City, Florida. 1949+ quarterly. Editors: Will Tullos, Evelyn
Thorne.

This is a carefully letterpressed poetry-only magazine important for its consistent openness and its longevity across
two eras of literary history. A full run through the sixties
(v.11 to v.20) gives an excellent scent of the decade. Special
issues include "108 Prayers for J. Edgar" by Will Inman (extra issue, 1965). Frontispiece illustrations are by Ben Tibbs,
Bethel Wilkinson, Barbara Galloway, and others. Each issue
publishes some two dozen contemporary poets.

The Fiddlehead. University of New Brunswick, Fredericton
(N.B.), Canada. 1945+. Editors: Donald Gammon, Robert
Rogers, Fred Cogswell (1945–53); Fred Cogswell (1953–
67); Kent Thompson, R. Gibbs, J. Zanes (1967–68); Kent
Thompson (1969–70).

The Fiddlehead, which was published for its first eight years
as a mimeo (1945–53), grew out of literary "meetings" in
Toronto and New Brunswick between Alfred G. Bailey, Roy
Daniels, and Robert Finch. In 1940, in New Brunswick,
Bailey helped to organize a group of writers into what was
called the "Bliss Carmen Society" (Bliss Carmen was one of
the writers). The society was dedicated to preserving the tradition of poetry in New Brunswick and, according to Bailey,
"To continue a tradition is to develop it to the point of con-

temporaneity." *The Fiddlehead* has sought, in the sixties, to broaden itself to include Canadian letters in general. "Half of the significant writing being done in Canada is being done in Fredericton, New Brunswick; the other half is being done elsewhere and is published in *The Fiddlehead"* (1970). Poets featured in the last ten years have been George Bowering, Michael Bullock, Louis Dudek, and Henry Beissel. Many Americans and others have also been published.

Floating Bear, A Newsletter. New York City (1961–69); San Francisco (1969). 1961+ irregular. Editor: Diane Di Prima.

Editor of the well-known Poets Press in upstate New York, Diane Di Prima published *The Floating Bear* as a revolutionary "newsletter" of poetry (see also her *Revolutionary Letters*). *The Floating Bear* is slightly more interested in social and political (than literary) experiment, but it belongs to— in fact *predates*—the sixties mimeo movement. Work has appeared by John Wieners, Jack Spicer, Gary Snyder, LeRoi Jones, Keith Wilson, Tom Clark, Clark Coolidge, Lenore Kandel, and Michael McClure.

Folio. Birmingham, Alabama. 1964+ triannual. Editor: Adele Sophie de La Barre.

This magazine has managed to publish consistently good work by local (Birmingham) writers alongside those from all over the country. It has featured an "undergraduate section" (prep school and college students only). Publishes poetry, fiction, and graphics. "Please avoid moralizing summaries," it tells prospective contributors. "We are subject to many contributions full of large words like 'eternity,' 'divinity.' Please, a minimum of such." Contributors include locals: J. Mitchell Pilcher, Frances Shillingburg, Amasa Smith Jr.; non-locals: Louis Newman, Leonard A. Casso, Gary Elder. Directory of contributors appears in volume 3, number 3, Winter 1967.

Foxfire. Rabun Gap, Georgia. 1967+ quarterly. Editor: B. Eliot Wigginton.

This magazine represents two important things: an early move on the part of the small presses in the interest of ecological harmony and do-it-yourselfism, and a deeply rooted local effort in a small southern town. "We are in as unlikely a place as Rabun Gap because that's one of the few places left in this country where the information we're interested in on total self sufficiency can still be found." *Foxfire* publishes poetry, articles, art, and photos. Its main power has been do-it-yourself features: planting by the Zodiac (v.1, no.2); Cherokee issue—history, medicines, foods, superstitions (v.1, no.3); moonshining (v.3, no.2). Excellent reproduction, many photos, good artwork.

Free Lance, A magazine of poetry and prose. Cleveland, Ohio. 1950 or 1952+ irregular. Editors: Casper Jordan (1950–67); Adelaide Simon, Casper Jordan, Russell Atkins (1967); Casper Jordan, Russell Atkins (1968–70).

Over the years the voice of Cleveland poets and those elsewhere, *The Free Lance* was, through the fifties, a publication of "The Free Lance Poets and Prose Workshop, Inc." It has been interested in experimental writing and has published prose, poetry, articles, reviews, criticism, and essays. During 1965 the late d. a. Levy served as art editor. Throughout the sixties *The Free Lance* published many contemporary writers, including Kent Taylor, John Cornillon, Paul Kemp, Jau Billera, and D. r. Wagner—all Clevelanders of one vintage or another. Volume 13, numbers 1 and 2 (1969), is a special "Simon Memorial" issue, with an article on the late Adelaide Simon by Russell Atkins.

Goliards. Tampa, Florida (1964–65); Milwaukee, Wisconsin (1966); San Francisco (1967–69); Bellingham, Washington (1969–70). 1964+ irregular. Editor: Jerry H. Burns.

This magazine, at the mercy of its peripatetic editor, represented a midwestern-southeastern brand of mid-sixties mimeo publishing. Now in the Northwest, it does less frequent and smart offset editions, and shows no longer any regional biases: "Intent on lively and literate creative expression, I need the new and unique—that which has not yet been formulated, therefore no editorial preconceptions or limitations. Crafted ecstasy swings." The latter sentence is typical of some of the editor's somewhat cryptic qualities. The magazine is also interested in mysticism, Tarot; has good artwork and photos as an offset production.

Grande Ronde Review. LaGrande, Oregon (1964–67); Sacramento, California (1967–70). 1964+ irregular. Editor: Ben L. Hiatt.

GRR arose in the midst of the mid-sixties mimeo movement and out of the northeastern Oregon poetry scene, which included *Blitz, The Middle R, Prensa de Lagar,* and *Pleigo.* For two issues it was edited by Michael Andrews; Ben L. Hiatt took over with number 3: "There are no longer any conservatives on the *GRR* staff; people with good sense and a conscience but not conservatives." By volume 2, number 1 ("finally starved out of that beautiful, isolated, sex-starved, hypocritical village"), Hiatt was producing *GRR* from Sacramento, and the range of his concern broadened. He became an offset printer, and his magazine went with him, changed too from 8½ by 11 to 7 by 8½ and finally to 5½ by 8½. Now he feels that "a little magazine should serve a revolutionary function and act as a vanguard." *GRR* has published Ron Bayes, Keith Wilson, Phil Whalen, Mel Buffington, Judson Crews, Lyn Lifshin, and Gene Fowler; and stories by Barbara Miller, Michael D. Lally, and Bill Kennedy. Latest issue (no.12, 1970) contains an editorial, "From the Bottom of the Bottle," reestablishing *GRR's* independence as a little magazine.

El Grito. Berkeley, California. 1967+ quarterly. Editors: Nick Vaca, Andred Ybarra.

This is a large, well-produced magazine "strongly oriented toward Mexican-American readers and those interested in the intellectual expression of Mexican Americans." Contains fiction, poetry, articles, art, reviews, photos, interviews, satire, criticism, and essays.

Gronk. Toronto (Ontario), Canada. 1965+ irregular. Editors: Several, including bp Nichol, David Aylward, David W. Harris, Rah Smith, Jon Riddell, Bill Bissett.

Published by the prolific offset-mimeo Ganglia Press, *Gronk* features concrete poetry by the above editors and others, including Joseph Di Donato, Steve McCafferty, and D. r. Wagner. It is "concerned with concrete sound kinetic and related borderblur poetry." *Gronk* series 2, number 3 (Nov. 1968) is a single sheet with the word "dead" calligraphed on it. Who knows? Books from Ganglia Press are as variegated and un-predictable as this magazine. Some productions are *Wourneys* by David Aylward, *Something In* by Martina Clinton, and *Sprouds and Vigables* by D. r. Wagner. Newsletters are also produced by Ganglia, clearly one of Canada's least sedentary presses. It is associated with Blew Ointment Press.

Hanging Loose. Brooklyn, New York. 1966+ quarterly. Editors: Ron Schreiber, Dick Lourie, Robert Hershon, Emmett Jarrett, Miguel Ortiz.

The forty-plus pages of this magazine literally hang loose in a 5½ by 8½ envelope which is printed as a cover. "We think this kind of free arrangement creates a sense of immediacy: you have each poem really by itself. Furthermore, to dispense with the notion that each poet's work should be somehow set in 'proper' order relative to the others . . . is to dispense with a kind of middleman; so that the relationship between the single poet and his reader becomes a more direct one." Early issues were mimeographed, later ones offset. *Hanging Loose,* in ten issues, has published work by Denise Levertov, John Gill, Dan Georgakas, Louis Ginsberg, and Lyn Lifshin.

Haravec, A literary magazine from Peru. Lima, Peru. 1966+ quarterly. Editor: Maureen Ahern Maurer.

This is a well-produced bilingual magazine (Spanish-English) of fiction, poetry, and translations. Number 2 (1967) contains contemporary Peruvian poetry and translations into English, plus several U.S. poets. Also included is a short story by Peru's José María Arguedas and photos of art work by Miguel Ángel Cuadros. Number 4 contains translations of anonymous Quechua poetry with notes by the translators. There is also an article by Mario Vargas Llosa, "Fate and Mission of the Writer in Latin America." Work by Charles Olson is also included.

Hearse. Eureka, California. 1957–61; resumed 1969||. Editor: E. V. Griffith.

Oddly enough, though this magazine is a significant eclectic force at both ends of the decade, it is for a sister publication, *Coffin,* that it is important to the mid-sixties. Published in 1964–65, *Coffin* was "an irregular portfolio in significant

163

new moulds, with each poem or drawing presented in an individual unit on colored stocks in a variety of colored inks and typefaces." *Coffin* included work by Charles Bukowski, Larry Eigner, Henry Miller, Gil Orlovitz, and Ben Tibbs. *Hearse,* consisting of poetry only, has published Dick Lourie, Hugh Knox, and George Thompson.

Hiram Poetry Review. Hiram, Ohio. 1966+ biannual. Editor: Hale Chatfield.

This magazine, formerly *Poetry Karamu,* is as important for its editorials and "correspondence" perhaps as for its poetry. "The business of poetry is, among other things, to restore to words and ideas, their original 'physicality,' " says the editor in number 6. "Poetry neither contains nor represents the truth; poetry *is* the truth," he says in number 8. Correspondence/commentary has appeared by Keith Wilson, Vassar Miller, and Peter Viereck. *Hiram Poetry Review* has published poetry by Russell Banks, Robert Lax, Charles Bukowski, Norman Hoegberg, and Art Cuelho.

Hors Commerce Press. Torrance, California. 1962–69||. Editor: James D. Callahan.

Though Callahan launched an all-prose magazine in 1966 (*Dypstych*) which only saw one or two numbers, it is for his excellent series of handset letterpress books throughout the sixties that he is known. These include *Five Poem Songs* by William Wantling, *Walt Whitman and the Kid in the Woodshed* by Ken Dobel, *A Birdness Flown* by Ben Tibbs, and *Sunset Beach* by Gerald Locklin.

Illuminations. Mill Valley, California (1965–68); El Rito, New Mexico (1969–70). 1965+ irregular. Editors: Norman and Hadassah Moser.

Though no issues have been produced since Winter 1968–69, this is a large, excellently produced magazine of poetry, articles, art, fiction, reviews, and comment. All but the last are in folio form. Number 1 measures 11 by 17; number 2, 10 by 14; numbers 3 and 4, 9 by 12. Number 2 contains Shaman songs by Gene Fowler, Norman Moser, Frank Melton. Number 3 has poetry by Douglas Blazek, William Margolis, and Gene Fowler. "The lyric . . . has of necessity merely changed. The necessity nowadays is to speak out as well as sing. The lyric narratives in prose and poetry . . . have of necessity expanded, allowing a more varied combination of elements."

Informer. Oxford, England. 1966+ quarterly. Editors: Keith Armstrong, David Gill.

"Freedom (love) concrete poetry (if it lives) translations RETHINK. Beat poetry—no verse. Only poetry. Publishing Czech poetry. Pro diggers freedom of words pads of love/ you and your pen/ me and mine . . ."

Intrepid. Buffalo, New York. 1964+ quarterly. Editor: Allen DeLoach.

The editor, who organized and chaired the 1970 conference of the Committee of Small Magazine Editors and Publishers in Buffalo, "grew up" on the Lower East Side of New York in the early sixties. He has, in fact, edited an anthology called *The East Side Scene* (Buffalo: University Press, S.U.N.Y., 1968). *Intrepid* is characterized by this early environment and remains consistently open to new work, "nonestablishment and nonacademic." Number 7 (March 1967) contains a letter from Walter Lowenfels to Allen Ginsberg, and poetry by Charles Bukowski, Diane Di Prima, and Tuli Kupferberg. Numbers 11–12 contain a "revolutionary birth" play by Hayward Allen and poetry by George Dowden, Ray Bremser, and Ted Berrigan. Number 16 is a special "poetry of Canada" issue containing "the young generation of poets now revitalizing their country's literature": Victor Coleman, David Rosenberg, Lionel Kearns, Pat Lowther, Seymour Mayne, and others.

Kauri. New York City (1964–67); Washington, D.C. (1968–70). 1964–70 (?). Editor: Will Inman.

An early and mid-sixties mimeo, *Kauri* used a "literary medium to express the flavor and texture of diverse human individuals in search of Self, sometimes emphasizing political contradictions as clue. . . ." In 1968 the editor threatened first to retire and then to merge *Kauri* with Paul Hirschhorn's *Penumbra.* Neither has happened. In the June 1970 issue (no.32) he says: *Kauri* 33 will probably be the last . . . as a literary magazine anyway. Lit mags, as separate from human movement growth, seem irrelevant for my own work." Always politically and socially conscious, Will Inman over the years published hundreds of contemporary poets, many letters, and short comments. His own editorial is always thoughtful and knowledgeable.

Kayak. San Francisco (1964–69); Santa Cruz, California (1969–70). 1964+ quarterly. Editor: George Hitchcock.

Kayak began at the front end of the small press movement in the sixties, publishing what it considered to be "the best poets now working in the United States and Canada." It is "particularly hospitable to surrealist, imagist and political poems," and welcomes "vehement or ribald articles on the subject of modern poetry." Though a sternly independent publication, *Kayak* mainstay poets are often members of the academy; yet through brilliant editorship (and cantankerous humor) Hitchcock never permits the magazine to be dry or stuffy. Poets published throughout the sixties included Vern Rutsala, Robert Bly, Felix Pollak, Robin Skelton, and Carol Bergé. In 1968, *Kayak* conducted a contest (with a $400 prize) for the best poem in English on the life and death of Ché Guevara. Number 19 was "printed on rifle and small-arms target paper rejected as substandard by the U.S. Defense Department." *Kayak* has published excellent woodcuts, collages, and drawings, and is well known also for letters, articles, and reviews of contemporary books of poetry.

Klactoveedsedsteen. Heidelberg, Germany. 1965+ irregular. Editor: Carl H. Weissner.

Published in "all languages," this magazine and press (*Panic*) belong squarely with the international multimedia movement (Something Else Press, N.Y.C.; Ganglia Press, Toronto, etc.). "Focus on cut-up (foldin) semantic cosmonaut gear, articles, art, photos. All issues accompanied by a tape. Tape experiments word-sound bruitage." *Klacto* has published Julien Blaine, J. F. Bory, Douglas Blazek, Claude Pelieu, and William Burroughs.

Kulchur. New York City. 1960–65‖ quarterly. Editor: Lita Hornick, with LeRoi Jones as contributing editor.

This is a transitional magazine expensively produced, whose new and highly visual approach probably helped stimulate the sixties small-press movement. It publishes poetry, fiction, criticism, articles, art, and photos, and features David Meltzer, Gerard Malanga, Joe Brainard, David Antin, Ted Berrigan, and many others. Number 17 carries "Corregidor" by LeRoi Jones; number 18 has an interview with Paul Goodman by Morgan Gibson; and number 19 has an outrageous, hilarious prose-poem called "Yoga Exercises" by Tom Veitch.

Labris. Lier, Belgium (1961–67); Antwerp (1968+). 1961+ trimonthly. Editors: Ivo Vroom (1961–67); Edmond Devoghelaere, Pierr Anthonissen (1968+).

Labris is a huge mimeograph publication (over 100 pages) "dedicated to the avant-garde. All material is experimental, partly concrete-kinetic, partly beat influenced." An article on "poejazz, the reluctant couple," appears by the editor in number 3-4 (July 1966). Several languages, including English, French, and German, are used.

Les Lettres. Paris. 1963+ irregular. Editor: Pierre Garnier.

"The Spatialist Review," this is a magazine in French in letterpress format publishing spatial and concrete poetry, and criticism of concrete poetry. Belongs to European movement of concretists (see *Approches, Bollettino Tool, Tlaloc,* etc.).

Lillabulero, Being a periodical of literature and arts. Chapel Hill, North Carolina (1967–68); Ithaca, New York (1969–70). 1967+ irregular. Editors: Russell Banks, William Matthews.

A large, handsome mixture of offset and letterpress production, *Lillabulero* contains fiction, poetry, reviews, articles, and photo folios. First several issues measured 9 by 14; by number 7 (Fall 1969), the size was 6 by 9, and the new subtitle was "A Journal of Contemporary Writing." Special issues include a "Dixie Underground" issue and an "Underground Railroad" issue. *Lillabulero* has also published pamphlets by Harland Ristau, Peter Wild, Robert Peterson, and others.

Lines. New York City. 1964–65‖ irregular. Editor: Aram Saroyan.

Lines, which published six issues, was oriented toward early concrete poetry and poets of the "C" group in New York City. It published the work of Ted Berrigan, Ron Padgett, Clark Coolidge, Robert Lax, Joe Brainard, and William Burroughs. It also included concrete poetry by bp Nichol, Dom Sylvester Houedard, and Aram Saroyan.

Litmus. Seattle, Washington (1966–67); Berkeley, California (1967–68). 1966–68‖ irregular. Editor: Charles Potts.

The editor, one of the northwestern mimeo poets of the middle sixties, came to Berkeley in late 1967 where he was an important local force in poetry readings and a sort of tribe seer. In the Northwest he was associated with such poets as Ben Hiatt and Carlos Reyes; in Berkeley with John Oliver Simon and Richard Krech of Noh Directions Press. "Herein lies Litmus," said Potts in an editorial in number 1, "borne (sic) of the evil genius of an uptight draft dodger and the antigenius of a chronic collector of ideas which are invariable (sic) abandoned before too much is done about them." Number 2 carries Gino Clay's locally infamous attack on poet Gene Fowler and virtually all of his San Francisco contemporaries. Number 3 carries Margaret Randall's "Cuba: Impressions Eight Years from Triumph." Work by John Sinclair, Chuck Carlson, Edward Smith, and Jack Large has appeared.

Loc; Lisn. Leeds (1965); London (1966). 1965–66‖ quarterly. Editors: John J. Sharkey, Sonia G. Sharkey,

Loc is a mimeo of "postconcrete poetry, i.e., covers field of semiotics/ computer poetry/ nonverbal poetry/ formalism/ para-dada—visual poetries; i.e., recent manifestations in Europe and Brazil, occasionally verging toward the Fluxus line, but more serious/academic than that group." *Lisn* is a 20 by 30 "international poster poetry magazine. Semiotic work/ typestracts/ computer texts/ music texts/ borderline material from concrete outwards. The first spatial poetry magazine devoted to visual poetry in Britain and the World."

Loc-Sheets. Leeds, England. 1966–67‖ irregular. Editor: Cavan McCarthy.

These are mimeo sheets of information about the small presses, started as a supplement to McCarthy's *Tlaloc* (which see). Stood for one or two years as an evolving supplement to the *Dustbooks Directory of Little Magazines.*

Magazine. New York City. 1963+ annual. Editor: Kirby Congdon.

A large mimeo that, whether the editor likes it or not, had much to do with the sixties mimeo movement. "Poetry that exploits ideas and emotions equally, and for a nonprofessional, nonliterary but intelligent audience. We encourage experiment, exposure, trial-and-error (rather than success and prestige per se)." Number 4 (1969) features motorcycle poems "to illustrate the editor's contention that poetry can and should extract itself from the lady's garden, the gentleman's parlor, and the academician's research library."

The Marrahwannah Quarterly. Cleveland, Ohio. 1964–68‖ irregular. Editor: d. a. Levy.

Sometime (before it was fashionable and before "ecology" got onto the market) in the slow, agonizing, and final death of Lake Erie, a group of Cleveland poets began to write protest poems about it, and about much else ill in Cleveland and the industrialized United States. This group included rjs, Kent Taylor, D. r. Wagner, and Adelaide Simon. But it included most of all d. a. Levy, the unsurpassed master of mimeo "poeteditorpublishing," who shot himself in November 1968, at the age of twenty-six. There is no fair way to deal with Levy's work in this space. Much of that work was so highly personalized in so few copies that we'll never know about it. The great bulk of it resides in the private files of friends. I doubt there is one librarian on earth who has had the foresight and plain guts to establish even a modest collection. Levy published issues of *MQ* as late as 1967–68 (no.14). He moved away from marijuana after busts and was busted (also) for "obscenity" at least once. Working mostly in mimeography, he had as his main lines of interest concrete poetry, collages and cut-ups, and political and social issues, local and national. He published under many imprints (7 Flowers Press, Ghost Press, Renegade Press, etc.), and some of the books were very substantial in length (see *Cleveland Concrete, Cleveland Undercovers,* or *465, An Anthology of Cleveland Poets*) and scope. *MQ* as an irregular periodical, however, is a good, if microcosmic, sample of his work as an editor or poet or publisher or, as he would have it, as a person. *MQ* number 2 (1964) quotes Voznesensky: "Poetry always means Revolution." That was the tone thereafter.

Mele, International Poetry Letter. Honolulu, Hawaii. 1965+ quarterly. Editors: Stefan Baciu, José L. Varela Ibarra.

This is a linguistically courageous poetry magazine—perhaps the *only* mag in Hawaii. *Mele* looks for "young American poetry with passion and guts to blend with the Asian, African, European and Latin-American poetry we publish. Are bland housewives and grandmothers the only people writing in the U.S.A. today?" In humble offset appearance, this is truly a poetry magazine of many languages, including some (transliterated) native Hawaiian. Special issues have included an anthology of poetry from Haiti, and young poets of Hawaii.

Midwest. Geneva, Illinois. 1960–66|| irregular. Editor: R. R. Cuscaden.

An important magazine of the early sixties, *Midwest* carried articles, art, reviews, interviews, photos, and criticism, all "stressing the region for which it is named; an unpublished poet from Cedar Rapids, for instance, has a better opportunity than a recognized poet from Buffalo . . . nevertheless, the basically untalented, the merely naive or the sadly facile get bounced fast—even if their postmark reads 'Oshkosh.' " Appealingly produced in its 5 by 7 letterpress format, *Midwest* published many important poets in the early sixties including Robert Bly, David Pearson Etter, Douglas Blazek, and Robert Sward.

The Montparnasse Review, A Magazine of Creative Writing. Paris. 1961–67 (?) irregular. Editors: Richard Banks, James Ryan.

Started as *Parnassus*, this letterpress magazine (in English) publishes poetry, fiction, and art. It has an international posture, few biases. Work by Daniel Mauroc, William Whitman, and Roy McNab has appeared.

Mt. Adams Review. Cincinnati, Ohio Art Association. 1959+ bimonthly. Editors: George Thompson, Tom McEvilley (literary ed.), Stanley Sulkes (public affairs ed.), Tom Oldendick (art ed.).

This excellent magazine spans the entire decade, always maintains an open view of literature and society. "Our Public Affairs Department has some regional and local interest.

In all areas we want to see the unpopular, the neglected, the advance guard, the provocative, the perverse. Craft, focus, and evidenced argument are important for nonfiction, including satire, which so many writers lately seem to think will excuse a lot." Poetry by Yasuo Sasaki, Victor Contoski, William C. Dell, and Judson Crews has appeared, and art by Hugo Mujica, Sylvia Roth, and Mary Acosta.

Nebulum. 1966–67‖ irregular. *Nebulum's Olive Dachshund.* 1968–69‖ irregular. Oxford, England. Editors: Glyn Pursglove, Philip Hodson (1966–67); Glyn Pursglove (1968–69).

This is an experimental mimeo which emphasizes experimental work and publishes fiction, poetry, articles, reviews, interviews, criticism, concrete poetry, and kinkon. "For experimental work: Black Mountain through to, and beyond, nonverbal, etc. For sound such visual as can be duplicated without too much loss; semiotics, simultaneous poetry, brutist poetry perhaps; computer poems, rhythm machines, arguments, theories, manifestos, news." Uses work by Gerhard Rühm of Austria, Jean-Marie Le Sidaner of France, and Jiri Valoch of Czechoslovakia.

New: American Canadian Poetry. Trumansburg, New York. 1966+ triannual. Editors: John Gill, Earle Birney, Patrick Lane.

This is an excellent review of current poets, U.S. and Canadian. It has carried work by Patrick Lane, Peter Wild, Tom Wayman, Eugene McNamara, Robert Hershon, Dick Lourie, and many others in twelve issues.

New Measure, A Magazine of Poetry. Oxford, England. 1965–68‖ triannual. Editor: Peter Jay.

This is a fine, "editorially eclectic" magazine whose "view is not merely contemporary, it is everything we make fresh for ourselves." In its ten issues, it published work by W. H. Auden, Christopher Middleton, Gavin Bantock, George Bowering, and George Dowden. Number 2 (1966) carried translations from German, French, Greek, and Russian. Number 6 (1967) is devoted to American poetry, including work by Gary Snyder, Edward Dorn, Clayton Eshelman, and Jerome

171

Rothenberg. It also includes Gail Turnbull's "Notes on Robert Duncan."

Nexus, The San Francisco Literary Magazine. San Francisco, California. 1963–65, January to March 1967‖ bimonthly. Editor: Jerome Kulek.

Jerome Kulek, a printer-publisher and sometime polemicist, picked up where *Genesis West, Contact,* and others had stopped, and for a couple of years published some of the best material in the Bay Area. In early 1967 he attempted a comeback, published a couple of issues and quit again. From time to time now, rumors slip out of the city that he is talking about a third go. *Nexus* was frantically independent, argumentative, always interesting. It published many articles, and regular contributions by Peter Edler and Robert Upton. Much fiction also appeared, including work by James D. Houston, Ed Bullins, and Edward Franklin. Many cartoons and covers appeared by B. Kliban. The magazine also featured satire, poetry, drama, and criticism.

Olé. Bensenville, Illinois (1964–66); San Francisco (1967). November 1964 to May 1967‖ triannual. Editor: Douglas Blazek.

This magazine was at the very heart of the sixties mimeo movement (the Mimeo Press was its publisher), and the most important, driving force in "meat poetry," which ran concomitant to mimeo movement. *Olé* was also a prime mover of such poets as Charles Bukowski, Steven Richmond, William Wantling, Harold Norse, T. L. Kryss, Brown Miller, and editor Blazek himself. *Olé,* and the movement it fostered in seven issues, was "dedicated to the cause of making poetry dangerous." Blazek's vision of poetry appears in *Olé* number 1: "Every inch of the planet Earth, every curse word, every thimble, every spot of dirt, every slam, bang, jing, every chug in the harbor is poetry . . . add the thumb screws with the raspberries and you have solid green earth: RE-AL-IT-Y." In number 6, *Olé* says it is "dedicated to all poetniks, lifeniks and the making of poetry into a dangerous meat-plasma that clogs our every deed and smears our every thought." Special issues include the work of Harold Norse (no.5) and "The Godzilla Review issue of Small Press Publications comprehensively encompassing books published over the last half decade" (no.7, May 1967).

Openings. Woodchester (Gloucester), England. 1964+ irregular. Editors: John Furnival, Dom Sylvester Houedard.

Largely operating as a press, *Openings* publishes concrete experimental poetry, poster poems, graphic scores, single sheets, cards, and folders containing up to twenty-four loose sheets. The press has published books by Hansjorg Mayer, Ronald Johnson, Ian Hamilton Finlay, John Furnival, and Edwin Morgan.

Outcast. Santa Fe, New Mexico. 1966–70‖ quarterly. Editors: Jean Rosenbaum, Veryl Rosenbaum.

The vision in this southwestern mimeo publication is that poets are outcasts. "In our century either the Poet is, by the external nature of society, an outright revolutionary or he is writing ancient history." In 1970 the editors quit, angrily concluding that American letters was "not worth it." During its four-year life *Outcast* published much good poetry, including work by Sanford Dorbin, William R. Lamppa, Louis Ginsberg, Lyn Lifshin, R. D. Lakin, and Ed Ochester.

The Outsider, A Book Periodical. New Orleans, Louisiana (1961–65); Tucson, Arizona (1966+). 1961–69 (?) annual. Editors: Jon E. Webb, Gypsy Lou Webb.

Published by the well-known Loujon Press, this magazine is one of the most elaborate among the independent little mags, printed by hand in letterpress, and handbound. Editors Jon and Gypsy Lou Webb put literally everything they had in number 4-5 which was published in early 1969. "Unless something quite unexpected comes our way, a substantial grant or private subsidy, this . . . issue is our last." None has appeared since, though rumor is that the Webbs will continue. Number 4-5 carries a special 46-page "homage to Patchen." Number 3 carries an editorial by Patchen, and cites Charles Bukowski as the "Outsider of the Year" (1962). Number 2 includes William S. Burroughs, Anselm Hollo, Walter Lowenfels, Jack Kerouac, Henry Miller, and two dozen others. *The Outsider* has been interested in contemporary writing "known as the 'new writing,' not beat but experimental avant garde. Little or no rhymed verse. No incidental prose." Loujon Press has published exquisite books, including one by Charles Bukowski and one by Henry Miller.

Poet and Critic. Iowa State University, Ames, Iowa. 1964+ triannual. Editor: Richard Gustafson.

In a handsome letterpress format in which contributors comment on each other's work, *Poet and Critic* carries poetry, articles, art, reviews, interviews, satire, cartoons, and criticism. Published by the Department of English and Speech, it is billed as "a gallery of verse, a workshop in print, a studio of thought." Over the years it has published work by Antoni Gronowicz, Menke Katz, Ted Kooser, and Hugh Fox.

Poetmeat 1963–66||. *PM Newsletter* 1967+ (?) triannual. Blackburn (Lancashire), England. Editors: Dave Cunliffe, Tina Morris.

This is an important British mimeo publication of the mid-sixties which attempts "comprehensive coverage of world avant garde w/exceptions. Bias toward continuing Romantic-lit-revolt/ expanding consciousness/ poet as prophet/ balance of form and content without sacrifice of either. An international underground mag bias against court jester entertainers and surface post-BM trappings, etc. to disguise lack of vision and (often) craft." Editor Dave Cunliffe was busted in Blackburn in 1965 upon publishing *Golden Convolvulus,* an anthology of erotica-poems, graffiti, children's rhymes, and press clippings of sex trials. *Poetmeat* has published work by Lee Harwood, Arthur Moyse, Peter Jay, Jim Burns, and William Wantling. Number 11 features underground commentary on Cunliffe's trial; number 12 is dedicated to "The Total Revolution."

Poetry Australia. Five Dock, Australia. 1964+ bimonthly. Editor: Grace Perry.

Published at the well-known South Head Press, *PA* is a nice-looking letterpress format of poetry, reviews, criticism, and interviews. It has an international posture but has also published many Australians, including Christopher Koch, Bruce Beaver, and Margaret Diesendorf. Special issues include: New Zealand poetry (no.9), West Australian poetry (no.12), Italian poetry (no.22-23), "Preface to the Seventies" (no.32), and "Captain Cook Bi-Centenary" (no. 33).

Poetry Newsletter. New York City (1964–66); Sacramento, California (1966–67). 1964–67‖ bimonthly. Editors: Wallace Depew, Linda Bandt.

This magazine is important for its involvement in the mid-sixties mimeo movement. Featuring poetry, letters, news, reviews, and essays, *PN* helped stimulate communication among young mimeo editors and publicized the small presses. "We are opposed to 'begging' poems from big-name poets because it degrades the poet (who often sends second rate material) and poetry (for people are ignorant enough to read it and believe it is good on the basis of who wrote it)." *PN* in twelve issues printed work by Stanley Fisher, Harvey Tucker, Michael Perkins, Susan Johnson, Eric Cashen, and Marcus Grapes. Wally Depew, now editor of *Dust,* has since published an excellent series of small, mimeo, nonverbal "experiments" (*PN2, PN3 series*) and is, in this country along with Something Else Press, a leading concretist.

Poesie Vivante, Le journal des Poetas, edité à Genève (1964). Tribune Internationale de Poésie (1965+). Geneva, Switzerland. 1964+ bimonthly. Editor: Pierre Marie.

This magazine is primarily in French, but texts are often multilingual. It carries poetry, articles, art, reviews, interviews, photos, criticism, and concrete poetry. The magazine actually represents an international society ("P.V. Groups") which "goes far beyond the magazine as such—a movement which is incontestably playing its part in the struggle for world peace and *rapprochement* between peoples." The editorial policy is "to develop a new humanism integrating poetry more and more into daily life and ensuring a place for it amongst international exchanges." Work by Ondra Lysohorsky, André Le Bois, and Josefina Pla has appeared.

Prism International. University of British Columbia, Vancouver (British Columbia), Canada. 1959+ biannual. Editor: Jacob Zilber.

This is a publication of the Creative Writing Department, University of British Columbia, which carries fiction, art, poetry, photos, interviews, satire, plays. Malcolm Lowry, Margaret Atwood, Paul Valery, Ivan Malinovsky, and Geraldo Sobral have all appeared.

Pyramid. Belmont, Massachusetts. 1968+ quarterly. Editor: Ottone M. Riccio.

This magazine, at first guided by a somewhat conservative aesthetic, has published some excellent work by Gary Elder, Emilie Glen, Ben Tibbs, Jerry Parrott, Sue Abbott Boyd, and Peter Wild. Number 6 is a special memorial issue to Helen C. Riccio.

Quixote. Madison, Wisconsin (1965–69); Lodz, Poland (1969–70). 1965+ monthly through 1969; now irregular. Editor: Morris Edelson (and occasional others).

One of the most important "magazines" of the mid- and late-decade, *Quixote* possessed the following proclivities: "Revolutionary writing with technical control or else so experimental even the artist is sincerely confused" (1966); "Experimental or well-controlled forms, to include concrete" (1968); "work or worker stories, reviews and commentary on all cultural subjects since we do a lot of theatre" (1969). The editor, an exacting printer-publisher and sometime teacher (now teaching English at the University of Lodz, Poland) worked massively over the possible ranges of modern publishing, from concrete, cut-up, cut-out, and collage work to the intermedium arts. No two of anything he published, magazine or book, were the same. Some were enormous projects, like Norbert Blei's *The Watercolored World* (Q. v.4, no.2) or the special University of Wisconsin Literary Contest winners issue (Q. v.4, no.5); some were diminutive —L. B. Delpino's *The Sparrow and the Cock* (Q. v.5, no.12) or the reprint of the *New Student* issue of March 1934 (Q. v.4, no.6) or *Quixote* volume 4, number 7 by M. Lesy. Poets published include Ed Ochester, Bob Watt, and James Bertolino. A special issue on the northwest poets (1968) is excellent.

Riverside Quarterly. Regina (Saskatchewan), Canada. 1964+ quarterly. Editor: Leland Sapiro.

This is a magazine for "literate readers of science fiction and fantasy," with emphasis on the critical aspects of that genre. It has featured "the Mystic Renaissance" in three parts by the editor ("A Survey of F. Orlin Tremaine's Astounding Stories") and work by Janet Fox, Jim Harmon ("The Seasonal Fan"), and Sam Moskowitz. It has treated Edgar Rice Burroughs, H. G. Wells, Ray Bradbury, and Kurd Lasswitz.

Runcible Spoon 1968+. *Moonstones* 1965–67||. *The Eight Pager* 1966–67||. *My Landlord Must Be Really Upset* 1970+. Niagara Falls, New York (1965–66); Sacramento, California (1967+). Irregular. Editor: D. r. Wagner.

These publications are as important for their editor as for themselves. D. r. Wagner is a sometime Clevelander and a friend of d. a. Levy. In the fashion of Levy, he has been a prolific mimeo publisher, vital in the mid-sixties mimeo movement. His publications (many books) and activities exist now, insofar as possible, in a community of friends whom he can know personally. *"Runcible Spoon* is communication, a place, a time/ for killing floor while waiting, a person, an idea, a way of life that involves publishing, talking, writing letters, making phone calls, taking walks, a place to rest, a concrete poem of all of us together, a gentleness, an attempt at being human." Wagner has moved to, and through, concrete and nonverbal poetry, and glass poetry. *The Eight Pager* was "a happening in eight parts" published in 1966, and included work by Carl Larsen, E. R. Baxter, Grace Butcher, Kent Taylor, Tuli Kupferberg, and others. *Moonstones* (four issues), "a magazine designed to be read by anyone desiring something to read while waiting for something to read," made the transition to *Runcible Spoon* in 1968.

Salted Feathers. Pullman, Washington (1964–65); Portland, Oregon (1965–69). 1964–69|| irregular. Editors: Dick Bakken, Lee Altman.

This is an important early mimeo of poetry whose final issue in summer 1969 was titled *Ginsberg/Portland*. An index through volume 3 was published in 1966 (together with a financial balance sheet for the first six issues). Poets published include Charles Bukowski, Pablo Neruda, Ping Hisn, Howard McCord, and Padraig Ó Broin. An interview with John Logan appears in number 7 (1966).

The Sixties 1958–69||. *The Seventies* 1969+. Madison, Minnesota. Irregular. Editor: Robert Bly.

This magazine, under the editorship of imagist poet Robert Bly, started in 1958 as *The Fifties,* became *The Sixties* in its proper decade, and is now called *The Seventies.* Most poems published try to be "composed almost entirely of images." Work by Galway Kinnell, David Ignatow, James Dickey, James Wright, and Louis Simpson has appeared. Number 9 carries "The Collapse of James Dickey" by Bly and much work by Miguel Hernandez. Number 10 has a section on "What Norwegian Poetry Is Like," with work by Olaf Bull, Henrik Ibsen, and Rolf Jacobsen.

Small Press Review. El Cerrito, California (1967–68); Paradise, California (1969–70). 1967+ irregular. Editor: Len Fulton.

Designed as a "trade" journal for small-press publishing and a quarterly up-dater for the *Annual Directory of Little Magazines, SPR* has defined itself closer to a journal of critical reviews on small press productions and news about the small-press scene in general. Number 1 is a memorial issue to the late Alan Swallow; number 4 features the inception of COSMEP (Committee of Small Magazine Editors and Publishers); number 5 features commentary on the work of poet Douglas Blazek by Joel Deutsch; and in number 6-7 the editor reviews the thrust of the small presses in the sixties. Review essays by Gary Elder, Douglas Blazek, Andrew Curry, Richard Morris, and many others have appeared.

The Smith. New York City. 1964+ biannual. Editor: Harry Smith.

The Smith, carrying the image of the anvil on its first cover, billed itself as "the strongest magazine." In 1965 it was "dedicated to generalism—uniting specialties, coordinating diverse events, from many sources creating large patterns, and a passionate and coherent world-view." Over the decade it grew steadily impatient with modern, complex society until, in 1970, though still "the strongest magazine," it is also "the enemy of civilization." It publishes much in the way of news and reviews on the culture. The editor, always cantankerous toward the Establishment, also publishes *The Newsletter on the State of Culture,* a tattle-tale sheet on the New York culture vultures. Much good creative material has appeared in *The Smith,* including work by H. L. Van Brunt,

David R. Bunch, Robert Chute, Lewis Turco, and Stephen Dwoskin.

Something Else Newsletter. New York City. 1966+ bi-monthly. Editor: Dick Higgins; also Emmett Williams (1966 and 1969); Arthur Craig (1967–68); Barbara Moore (1966).

The *Newsletter* is "essentially to promote development of critical attitudes and concepts appropriate to happenings and other avant garde works that fall in between conventional media." Something Else Press, which publishes the *Newsletter,* is noted for its unusual, craftsmanlike hardcover books and its Great Bear pamphlet series earlier in the decade. The editor is interested in happenings, intermedia, and nonverbal work. He is in spiritual (and in some measure financial, since he distributes their books in the United States) fraternity with the European concretists.

South and West, An International Literary Quarterly. Ft. Smith, Arkansas. 1962+ quarterly. Editor: Sue Abbott Boyd.

Throughout the sixties *S&W* has been the voice of the central South—and remains so now—engaging in all manner of cultural activities there. The magazine is only the tip of the iceberg that has been a huge publishing venture. In addition to enormous local participation, work by poets throughout the world has been published.

Tangents. Los Angeles, California. 1965+ bimonthly. Editor: Don Slater.

This is a slick magazine published by the Tangent Group and contains poetry, articles, fiction, art, reviews, photos, interviews, satire, criticism, cartoons, and letters. It is "limited to items concerning sex, primarily homosexuality or censorship."

Tlaloc. London, England. 1964+ irregular. Editor: Cavan McCarthy.

This is an important British mimeo publication which belongs to the international nonverbal poetry movement (see also *Approches, Bollettino Tool, Klactoveedsedsteen,* etc.). The editor throughout the decade committed himself to information about, and communication between, concretists from many countries. *Tlaloc,* "an international mag of modern poetry and experimental texts, chiefly noted for visual/concrete poems," has published Ian Hamilton Finlay, Vladimir Burda, Jiri Valoch, Patrick Hughes, and many others.

Trace. Los Angeles, California. 1952–70 triannual. Editor: James Boyer May.

Trace, important over two decades (and 70-plus issues) for excellence of material, design, and production, picked up early in the sixties on the information aspects of the small presses and issued an "evolving directory" with each issue. Perhaps the world's foremost expert on the little magazine, James Boyer May is now an associate editor for Dustbooks' *Directory of Little Magazines and Small Presses. Trace* has published much good poetry and fiction, good reviews, letters, and essays. It seeks "work indicating development of valid individuality." Hundreds of writers and artists contributed to it throughout the sixties. J. B. May was an editor of *The International Guide* (1960), and in many ways his evolving directory is an extension of that.

University of Tampa Poetry Review. Tampa. Florida. 1964+ quarterly. Editor: Duane Locke.

Few, if any, little magazines in the decade of the sixties publish more poetry than this one. Having a "preference for linguistic reality—a self-contained interior cosmos," Locke manages to keep his pages open to almost all types of material. (Number 17 has an essay by him on poetry as "an art of the superconscious.") Since 1964 *Poetry Review,* in its large offset format (it began as a mimeo), has published work by Jerome Rothenberg, Richard Deutch, Theodore Enslin, Erik Kiviat, Alex Silberman, and literally hundreds of others.

Western World Review. Culver City, California. 1965+ quarterly. Editor: Robert E. Sagehorn.

This is an unusual nonfiction magazine of relatively open editorial posture. It deals largely with politics, economics, media, and philosophy. The editor usually writes the entire issue (he also puts out a supplementary newsletter). The magazine has treated "The New Politics," "The McLuhan Galaxy," commentary on the western *Zeitgeist,* and "Latin and North American Culture Differences," by Hugh Fox.

Wild Dog. San Francisco, California. 1963–66|| ten per year. Editors: Drew Wagnon, Gino Clays.

This was an important, gutsy mimeo of the early and middle sixties. In many ways a precursor to the mimeo movement more than a member of it, *WD* seems to have quit during the peak of activity (early 1966), apparently its independence threatened. Its vintage seems to have been more in the Ed Sanders-Aram Saroyan era. In over twenty issues it published work by Robert Kelly, Edward Dorn, Margaret Randall, Larry Eigner, Joe Nickell, Gerard Malanga, and many others.

The Wormwood Review. Storrs, Connecticut (1959–69); Stockton, California (1969–70). 1959+ quarterly. Editor: Marvin Malone.

This magazine has had both a chronological and aesthetic range as great as any small magazine of the sixties. The editor, a professor of pharmacy, was one of Charles Bukowski's earliest publishers. "Still non-beat, non-academic, non-sewing circle and non-profit . . . interested in quality poems or prose-poems (proems) of all types—the form may be traditional or avant-garde-up-through-Dada, the tone serious or flip, the content conservative or utter taboo. We are not afraid of either wit or intelligence—they are rare qualities." Information broadsides are periodically included in the magazine. Christopher Perret, James Ryan Morris, Clive Matson, Simon Perchik, and Anne Waldman have appeared.

Zeitgeist. Saugatuck, Michigan. 1966+ quarterly. Editors: Gary Groat, Jean McCollom (associate editor).

This is a publication with irreverence even for itself. The editor is a fierce independent bordering on intellectual reclusion. He is an inveterate essayist, always outspoken. "Art is a beautiful lie, religion is a comforting lie, politics is a convenient lie. . . . The poems and stories in *Zeitgeist* are not meant as portrayals of reality, but as an interpretation of it—lies that may or may not lead us to knowledge and wisdom." *Zeitgeist* has published work by Ed Ochester, Robert Vander Molen, Ken Lawless, A. Quinn Smith, Sam Elkin, and many others. Many books have been published under the *Zeitgeist* imprint, mostly poetry and drama.

181